PRAISE FOR *LIFE STARTS NOW*

"If you are at a crossroads or a tipping point; if you are successful, yet empty; if you feel sad about the way life turned out and need to chart a way forward, look no further. You have found a trustworthy guide in Chanel. She is one of the wisest people I know. *Life Starts Now* is timely, accessible, and exactly what you need as you evaluate your priorities, pursuits, and purpose. You don't have to suffer in silence or settle for less. You don't have to overwhelm your heart or schedule looking for significance. You can find contentment where you are, on the way to where you are going. This book will help you embrace the truth and create the future you need."

—ASHLEY ABERCROMBIE, PODCAST HOST AND AUTHOR OF
RISE OF THE TRUTH TELLER AND *LOVE IS THE RESISTANCE*

"From the outside it appears we have it all. On the inside we fear we're missing out on our own lives. Chanel has an action plan. She guides our souls from exhaustion to nourishment. After absorbing her tactical wisdom, your life will officially be in session."

—AMY JO MARTIN, FOUNDER OF RENEGADE GLOBAL,
NEW YORK TIMES BESTSELLING AUTHOR, AND MOM

"Most of us live with a sense of angst, either deep below the surface or screaming in our face. For many this results in paralysis and further disappointment about how our lives have turned out. Angst and frustration can be used to fuel and discover our calling and redeem the broken parts of our lives. But it takes a leader with insight and wisdom to help you make that happen. And help is what Chanel so skillfully and beautifully does in this book. Chanel is equal parts wise guide, empathetic friend, and skilled practitioner, as she shows us how to channel frustration and uncertainty into calling and purpose. *Life Starts Now* will heal and awaken many hearts to the life they have been longing for. This book will be a profound gift for years to come."

—JON TYSON, AUTHOR AND PASTOR OF
CHURCH OF THE CITY NEW YORK

"Chanel Dokun has helped hundreds of women find their life's true purpose. In *Life Starts Now* she shares the overarching trends she's noticed in her years of life coaching—the trip-ups, the limiting beliefs, the lies we tell ourselves. Then she proceeds to walk the reader through her own coaching session. Dokun's insights are sharp; her writing is gorgeous. A truly thought-provoking, life-altering read!"

—GINA HAMADEY, FOUNDER OF PENKNIFE MEDIA
AND AUTHOR OF *I WANT TO THANK YOU*

"This book is hitting at the core of every meaningful conversation I am having with friends these days. Chanel found a way to give words to our foggy dialogue. This is the book I will send to all those friends."

—JEFF SHINABARGER, FOUNDER OF PLYWOOD
PEOPLE AND AUTHOR OF *LOVE OR WORK*

"From a young age I was taught that if you love what you do, you'll never work a day in your life—as if knowing what you love is easy. In *Life Starts Now* Chanel has given us one of the most honest and eloquent descriptions of how challenging it is to figure out who you are and what you want. With humor, wisdom, and clarity she guides us through letting go of the life we *should* live to experience the freedom of the life we most long for."

—DANA SPINOLA, FOUNDER OF FAB'RIK AND
AUTHOR OF *LOVE WHAT YOU DO*

"'It's not enough to keep you from drowning; I want to teach you how to swim.' It is this line among many that settled so deeply into my soul. As a guide, confidant, fellow traveler, and at times—dare I say—even a friend, Chanel Dokun not only offers so bold a sentiment, she delivers. *Life Starts Now* is legitimately one of the most grounded and helpful books I have ever read, and I genuinely believe—if you take her words to heart—this book will start you on your journey to cultivating a meaningful, rich, and purpose-filled life. God never intended for us to feel as though we were drowning in our own lives; Chanel shows us how to keep our heads above water and swim toward a glorious finish."

—LÉONCE B. CRUMP JR., COFOUNDER OF RENOVATION
CHURCH AND AUTHOR OF *RENOVATE*

"I've spent much of my life walking alongside women, encouraging and equipping them to create positive social change through building purposeful businesses. In Chanel, I've found a kindred spirit, fiercely committed to helping women become powerful leaders by owning their average and living courageously. With humor, wisdom, and a little bit of pluck, *Life Starts Now* is a must-read for any woman who wants to build a purposeful life."

—LIZ FORKIN BOHANNON, FOUNDER OF SSEKO DESIGNS AND AUTHOR OF *BEGINNER'S PLUCK*

"Chanel is the friend and cheerleader you didn't know you needed, and she might just change your life. Warm, funny, relatable, and wise, she's written a book that will challenge you to rethink your routines and refine your purpose, so that you can stop performing your life and start *living* it in a way that is true to your authentic self."

—CATHERINE PRICE, FOUNDER OF SCREENLIFEBALANCE.COM AND AUTHOR OF *HOW TO BREAK UP WITH YOUR PHONE* AND *THE POWER OF FUN*

life starts NOW

HOW TO CREATE THE LIFE YOU'VE BEEN WAITING FOR

CHANEL DOKUN

NELSON
BOOKS

An Imprint of Thomas Nelson

Published in Nashville, Tennessee, by Nelson Books, an imprint of Thomas Nelson. Nelson Books and Thomas Nelson are registered trademarks of HarperCollins Christian Publishing, Inc.

Thomas Nelson titles may be purchased in bulk for educational, business, fundraising, or sales promotional use. For information, please email SpecialMarkets@ThomasNelson.com.

Unless otherwise noted, Scripture quotations are taken from the Holy Bible, New International Version®, NIV®. Copyright © 1973, 1978, 1984, 2011 by Biblica, Inc.® Used by permission of Zondervan. All rights reserved worldwide. www.zondervan.com. The "NIV" and "New International Version" are trademarks registered in the United States Patent and Trademark Office by Biblica, Inc.®

Scripture quotations marked NLT are taken from the Holy Bible, New Living Translation. Copyright © 1996, 2004, 2015 by Tyndale House Foundation. Used by permission of Tyndale House Ministries, Carol Stream, Illinois 60188. All rights reserved.

Most client names have been changed and stories summarized to honor and protect individual identities.

Library of Congress Cataloging-in-Publication Data

Names: Dokun, Chanel, 1983- author.
Title: Life starts now : how to create the life you've been waiting for / Chanel Dokun.
Description: Nashville, Tennessee : Thomas Nelson, [2022] | Includes bibliographical references. | Summary: "Certified Life Planner and Relationship Expert Chanel Dokun shows women how to leave behind the stress and disappointment of a life spent chasing external significance and success and find profound joy and fulfillment in building a new one rooted in living out your unique purpose"-- Provided by publisher.
Identifiers: LCCN 2022003321 (print) | LCCN 2022003322 (ebook) | ISBN 9781400231294 | ISBN 9781400231355 (ebook)
Subjects: LCSH: Christian women--Religious life. | Self-actualization (Psychology)-- Religious aspects--Christianity. | Vocation--Christianity.
Classification: LCC BV4527 .D635 2022 (print) | LCC BV4527 (ebook) | DDC 248.8/43--dc23/eng/20220404
LC record available at https://lccn.loc.gov/2022003321
LC ebook record available at https://lccn.loc.gov/2022003322

Printed in the United States of America

22 23 24 25 26   LSC   5 4 3 2 1

*To my mother, Johnnie, who always helped
me keep my head above water.*

Contents

part one

DROWNING
IN SHALLOW
WATER

one

WHAT IT FEELS LIKE TO DROWN

Live as a stone in rushing water,
grounded no matter the current.

MORGAN HARPER NICHOLS, *ALL
ALONG YOU WERE BLOOMING*

Before we get into all the strategies, can we talk about how miserable you are? I mean, not outwardly or anything. By all appearances, you're doing fine. You've put on pants today, for goodness' sake, and your hair looks fantastic. Let's not be dramatic.

You're not miserable in an *I can't get out of bed* sort of way— okay, maybe sometimes in that way—but in the way a toddler is two tears from a tantrum after discovering their apple juice is sugar-free. They have a sneaking suspicion something is off, and they'd like to speak to the manager. "Where is the sugar? Where is the blast of joy?" *God, a little help, please.*

You've probably been miserable for a while. You didn't notice at first. School kept you busy—term papers, gossip, and making out in back seats occupied your attention. Or maybe that was just me. Later the freedom of early adulthood served as an appropriate distraction from the angst. I mean, IKEA furniture doesn't assemble itself. Who has time for a breakdown when a KALLAX shelving unit needs to be built?

But as you rounded thirty, settled into your career path, and dabbled in romances, the misery started to edge out the illusion of joy. You've had heartbreaks, deaths, disappointments, and betrayals. You were hired and then quit and then were fired for no good reason. Someone lied about you. A good friend forgot to send you a party invitation. A reality TV star was elected president. It might feel as though you are headed toward a midlife crisis, running into greater uncertainty.

But here's the good news.

You are not alone. Everyone around you is probably a little miserable too.

They, like you, are good at hiding it. They obscure their misery behind filtered Instagram pictures of exotic vacations, luxurious dinner parties, and "kids say the darndest things" photos of their children. But inside they are suffocating. I know this, not from conjecture or wishful thinking. I know because they tell me.

I'm the founder of Women of Consequence, an organization that helps women step into their life's true calling. For nearly a decade I've used my training as a life planner and therapist to guide women out of confusion and into clarity so they can live centered in their unique life purpose. For years women have come into my office, and after consent forms are signed, promises of therapist confidentiality are made, and purses are heaped on tables, they begin to remove the veneer.

They say things like:

- "I feel like I have no ownership over my life. I'm totally controlled by my responsibilities." Wanda was just about to turn thirty and was living single in New York City. After a recent promotion into a managerial position at her firm, she spent most of her time working long hours and trying to squeeze in time with friends around client deliverables and the odd online date. She told me, "I'm afraid one day I'm going to wake up and realize my whole life has passed me by."

- "I worry I'm not doing enough for God." Aubrey was drowning in shame. She wanted to work in the entertainment industry but couldn't see how that life could integrate her faith. So she kept going to a dead-end job that paid well but killed her passion. In our second session she confessed, "I know logically God loves me, but I don't feel it. I don't even know if I can trust him. I'm super involved in church, but sometimes it feels like I'm going through the motions. I wonder if God even has any big dreams for my life. Or are all the things I want in conflict with the life he thinks I should settle for?"

- "I hate my husband," Justine admitted. "We got married because I was pregnant and worried what people would think. But we're entirely the wrong fit. Now I feel trapped. Work used to help me ignore how unhappy I am with him, but now it's just me and the baby home all day until he shows up wanting dinner or sex. I hate my life. The hardest part is, I can't tell anyone how unhappy I feel. Most of my friends are single and keep telling me how lucky I am to have found someone. I've got it all—the kid, the house, the husband. What do I have to complain about?"

- "I always feel like I don't have enough time." Miriam dropped down on my sofa, breathless and stressed, rushing into the session ten minutes late. "Every day is like this marathon, running from one thing to the next, and none of it even matters to me. Wherever I am, I'm thinking about the next place I have to go. People keep talking about finding work/life balance—I just want a life. How am I so busy doing so much I don't love?"

- "I don't know how I'm going to pay for rent next month." Danielle was famous. Well, Insta-famous. She had a hundred thousand followers and big influencer contracts with brands, and she traveled three weeks out of every month. People hung on her every word as she broadcast her model life online. When we finally connected, she confessed, "I'm working so hard and everything looks so great online. But I have nothing in the bank. My boyfriend and I are fighting all the time because I never have enough time for him. I'm tired. I just keep waiting for the other shoe to drop."

They all cry. Gently at first, still holding it together. But soon even that effort feels beyond them, and they crumple into a puddle of regret, disillusionment, and despair right before my eyes.

I don't speak at first. Not even to offer tissues. Maybe it's the New Yorker in me, but I feel we should all have a little more license to ugly-cry in public. I wait. I hold on to their pain in silence, honoring the sacredness of their self-revelation. Sometimes that moment alone means everything—to be able to sit in sadness, free to admit without fear of judgment how unhappy they feel. Empathy can be a life vest for a woman who is drowning.

Which reminds me—before we move on, let me throw a life vest your way as well. If you feel like you're drowning, you truly are not alone. You're not the only one who hasn't figured out how to make life work. I know you feel insane at times, but know that you're not crazy. It makes sense that you feel the way you do. All that emotion—the sadness and disappointment, the fear and anxiety—is a warning sign. Emotions are like shots fired in the dark to let us know it's time to pay attention because something important is happening. Stop judging yourself and take note of what you're feeling. What might your emotions be trying to tell you?

For my clients, a common message tends to emerge. Their emotions illuminate the misalignment of their lives. We find that the lives they are living publicly are costing them something in private. In some cases, the price is self-respect. For others, it is time, relationships, or energy. But for everyone, chasing the good life means a loss of identity. They are increasingly disconnected from their core selves. And their emotions scream, *I can't afford to live this way anymore!*

So after acknowledging the discontent, we spend our time together trying to figure out what is at the root of the problem. If everything looks so great on the outside, but inside my clients are drowning, what is going wrong? To get to the bottom of it, I need to figure out each woman's mindset—to understand her anxieties, put language to her experience, and pull her head above water.

Luckily, I know exactly what it feels like to drown.

WHAT IT FEELS LIKE TO DROWN

1989

I'm drowning. Head fully submerged with arms flailing and breath diminishing. I am drowning quite publicly, in a kiddie pool at Wild Rivers in Southern California. I don't know how to swim, and at six years old I have already landed on the through line for what will become years of future therapy: I hate my mother for putting me in this position. I knew that coming to this water park with strangers was a bad idea—I don't even swim—but I had gone against my better judgment.

My bubble-printed, bathing-suited butt is high in the air. It's all anyone can see as I thrash about, trying to get my bearings below the surface. They must think I'm having fun. I bet the adults are even smiling, oblivious to my agony. *Look at her making a splash. She must be having a blast.* It's embarrassing, really.

Even at six I sense there is something shameful in the struggle. Where did I learn that? How did I come to believe my discomfort equaled inadequacy? Why do I feel guilty for my own suffering? Why will no one help me?

I start to swallow the water, taking in the chlorine-laced blue-green that surrounds me. It's proving to be an ineffective strategy. Aware my little body cannot contain the gallons of water of the pool, I fear I might drown from the inside out. I abandon the effort.

And then it happens. Call it physics. Call it Jesus. Call it the distant sound of laughter serving as a GPS. I don't know, but I realize I'm technically on my feet. This reorientation reminds me all I need to do is try to stand higher. I have been bent over all along, crouched low in an unnatural position. Could it be so simple?

I hoist my upper body onto my hands, downward dogging myself into a more stable state and then quickly, desperately, ease back onto my heels while I lift my body out of the water. No one notices my relief, except perhaps a little girl nearby who also seems to be recovering from her own glorious battle with a potential self-induced water death. She stands as well, pausing to center herself. Did she mouth "namaste" to me? Maybe. Well, my fellow water yogi, "The light in me recognizes the light in you too," I mouth as we both inch our way to the side of the pool. We are done playing for today.

Do you know what it feels like to drown in shallow water? I don't mean a brush with death at a water park. May the Lord spare you that indignity! You know what I'm talking about. You haven't been cheeks-up in a kiddie pool, head under a foot of water. But you know what it feels like to live in a perpetual state of trying to keep your head above the surface. From the outside everyone thinks you've got it together, but inside you feel like you're missing out on your own life.

The job you landed doesn't feel meaningful. There are glass ceilings everywhere you look. And even if you could break through, you're not sure you want what's on the other side. Your family is a disappointment. Don't get me wrong; they are lovely people. Well, some of them. But gatherings often leave you feeling misunderstood and disconnected in the very place you're meant to call home. Sex helps on occasion. Drinking numbs the ache for a time. But no matter how much effort you expend, the good life never seems to deliver on its promises. Sound familiar?

You try harder. Maybe a new career would shake things up for you. More money to buy more stuff to scratch that itch of insignificance. A bigger house might do the trick or maybe that beauty routine a twenty-year-old influencer posted on YouTube. Perhaps a new look could unlock your whole life's fulfillment. You suspect that's not true, so you go to church in search of something deeper. The service is a weekly reprieve from the misery of your regular rhythm. But the Sunday night blues are real. Before the worship songs have left your lips, you're already imagining how the perfect eyebrow arch or losing that last five pounds could fast-track your path to transcendence. Or so you think.

And so you strive.

And push.

And fight.

And it's all so exhausting. Most days, despite all the good and glorious moments, life feels most like treading water.

I wrote this book for women who are drowning. Or at least who feel like they are drowning when appearances suggest everything's going swimmingly well. And because I love you terribly, I have already given you the answer. The secret to saving yourself from drowning in shallow water is to stand up fully and breathe. By that I mean standing fully in the truth of who God has created you to be, facing your life for what it is, and finding joy there. This takes courage because it is far easier to live someone else's version of the good life than to live your own.

I find living to be like learning most anything. We first mimic what we see—like elementary school children tracing letters on a page. But eventually we have to abandon the template if we want to write our own story. I call this having the courage to be nobody. It's choosing to live against a blank slate where you write your life to be unlike anyone else's. It's paradoxical, as most of the great truths are. We become more by choosing to be nothing we've seen.

I'm going to show you how to stop drowning in shallow water because it sounds simple but is harder than we realize.* We'll get specific because I'm the kind of woman who Googles "how to boil a seven-minute egg" on a quarterly basis. I need instructions, folks, and clear action steps to follow. My husband will have them write, "She never met a manual she didn't love" on my tombstone. So I will make the process clear for those of you who don't need another flowery self-help book that inspires you but then leaves you stuck. I'll share my story of standing up, as well as anecdotes from the many clients I've served through the years in therapy and life planning who also came to this critical moment.

By the end of this book, I pray you will have a firm grasp of your unique life purpose. Because when we talk about being courageously like nobody else, we're really talking about finding the purpose you alone have been placed on this earth to fulfill. Use this book like a personal guide to help you let go of living the *should*-life and follow along as it leads you back to yourself.

---

* Isn't that the case with most things? Anyone who has assembled an IKEA BILLY bookcase knows simple doesn't equal easy.

We'll talk about the water. We'll acknowledge what it feels like to drown. And I'll teach you how to stand.

But first let me tell you how we all found ourselves bottoms-up in the shallow end of the good life.

two

THE PROBLEM WITH
CHASING SIGNIFICANCE

And what do you benefit if you gain the
whole world but lose your own soul?

MATTHEW 16:26 NLT

I've come to the conclusion that most women drown in shallow water because they are trying to lead extraordinary lives. Or as one writer put it, "People are suffering and dying under the torture of the fantasy self they're failing to become."[1] Women want to be exceptional. And before we rush to judgment, know that this unicorn complex isn't always ego-driven in the way one might think.

Some might say the search for significance is about expansiveness, trying to grow and push beyond limits to be the best of the best. While that may at times be true, I don't find that to be the case with most of my clients. I often start a coaching session by telling women they *aren't* special, and they breathe a sigh of relief as if they just got permission to give up the charade. Call it gender stereotyping, but posturing might be more of a male instinct.

Instead, when I work with women, I see their striving as desperate attempts to find outside of themselves what they wish they could feel inside. It's external identity formation rather than internal. Please catch this: *Ambitious women aren't always competing to beat an opponent, but more often to reconnect to the self.* They desperately want to come alive. So they strive and push to make something of themselves in order to feel whole. The problem is that self-actualization is an inside job. You can't succeed if you try from the outside in; you will lose every time.

Before we get into the cost of this external search for significance, let's take a detour through the common traps I see women falling into in order to feel successful. What limiting beliefs do women hold on to that keep them chasing significance outside of themselves?

LIMITING BELIEF #1: "I AM WHAT I DO"

Most women who reach out to me start by asking, "What am I supposed to do with my life?" And what they mean by that is "What job should I do?" This is a modern evolution of the concept of vocation. The question of calling used to be a spiritual quest to uncover who you are meant to be. Parker J. Palmer so eloquently captures this in *Let Your Life Speak*: "Vocation does not come from a voice 'out there' calling me to become something I am not. It comes from a voice 'in here' calling me to be the person I was born to be, to fulfill the original selfhood given me at birth by God."[2]

In our time, vocation is wholly summed up as #careergoals.

Move over, Christianity and Buddhism. In our post-postmodern society, work is the religion of choice. I'm not the first to notice this shift.

Many people have delved into this trend toward workaholism, but Derek Thompson has provided one of the clearest anthropological exposés of our culture in this area. In his article for the *Atlantic*, Thompson referred to the contemporary obsession with career as "workism." He defined this quasi-religious devotion as "the belief that work is not only necessary to economic production, but also the centerpiece of one's identity and life's purpose." Work, Thompson claims, has become the primary space where we expect to achieve transcendence, community, and a stronger sense of our own identity.[3]

Whoa. That's a lot of pressure to place on flipping burgers at McDonald's. Heck, that's a lot of pressure to attach to preparing briefs at a law firm or saving lives as a doctor. One of my early jobs was working as a hostess for the Cheesecake Factory, seating guests and cleaning menus. I love cheesecake with all my heart, but I don't know if working in a restaurant offered me transcendence. I don't think the Cheesecake Factory even offered me health insurance. But I digress.

Our cultural experience reaffirms this work-as-religion phenomenon. Think about it: What is the first question people tend to ask when they first meet one another? After names and greetings are exchanged, it's common for the first question to be "What do you do for a living?" We understand this question to mean "What is your job title?" or "What career path are you on now?" But imagine all the ways we could answer that question.

My job is perhaps the least substantial part of how I "make a living." Most days I make a life by drinking coffee first thing after writing in my journal or reading my Bible. I spend an inordinate amount of time scrolling through social media and responding to emails. I help my son with his homework and do yoga with my friend Meg. I worry about the state of the world and try to donate money to charities making an impact in spaces I can't help directly. Sometimes I see clients or look for ways to catalyze the women in my sphere of influence toward purposeful action. If I'm not too tired, I make love to my husband after eating dinner and putting our son to bed. How about you? How do you make a living?

There is nothing wrong with loving your work or building a successful career. In the garden, one of the first things Adam and Eve were given to do was a job.* But work needs to sit in its proper place. When work is a means of "identity production" versus "material production," as Thompson noted in his survey of millennial work life—*Houston, we have a problem*—we risk losing the edges to our workday, sacrificing our lives on the altar of a career. To become a workaholic is to become stuck in a loop of trying to prove one's value through doing.

Earlier I mentioned Wanda who came to me for a life plan after a big promotion at work. She complained of having no time for herself and hating her job, even though she was excellent at what she did. She also mentioned feeling frustrated by her friends who were always asking too much of her time, and she wanted more romance in her life.

When we did her life assessment, the elephant in the room was that she was working fourteen-hour days. Sometimes it was because the projects at hand called for that kind of output. But

---

* The Theology of Work Project has produced a fantastic set of articles around developing a holy vision for work. If you wrestle in this area, visit https://www.theologyofwork.org.

most of the time, those long hours at the office were self-inflicted. She could have put off tasks for the next day or delegated more to her juniors. But instead she routinely allowed work to take over and steal her evenings.

When we unpacked why she had trouble holding the boundaries of the workday, we discovered she had a limited view of her identity. For most of her life she had been an overperformer and gained success by the work of her hands, whether it was homework for school or projects at work. She didn't know herself outside of *doing*. She stayed at work long hours because that's where she felt most like herself. In friendships or out on dates, she was awkward and uncomfortable. She'd ask, "What is this time for? What am I supposed to be *doing*?"

If you're like Wanda, hear me on this: Your career is insufficient to bear the weight of your life purpose. Full stop. If you're struggling to find meaning in life, it's likely because you're looking for the whole of it in one place. It's like trying to make sense of an elephant by examining its tail. Sis, step back and expand your vision. You are more than your job.

Don't think so? Consider the five primary life buckets that contain who you are:

1. **CAREER.** You already know this one. It's how you make money and create products, services, or ideas.
2. **SELF.** This is the sacred space where only you reside, and it includes your personal health on physical, emotional, and psychological levels.
3. **RELATIONSHIPS.** Family, friends, and acquaintances occupy your time and energy in this bucket. It's where you are known.

4. **SPIRITUALITY.** This space is where you decenter the self and actively recognize you are a participant in a larger story.

5. **GLOBAL ENGAGEMENT.** Lastly, this is where you make a difference, whether it be locally or in the world at large.

All of these parts make up your individual identity, and all of them collectively hold your purpose. To be fulfilled, you have to move beyond work as the sole source of your significance. You are bigger than your career. Don't play small.

LIMITING BELIEF #2: "I AM WHO I LOVE"

Work isn't the only place women seek significance. Relationships are also an area of tension. After talking about work, women will usually ask, "How do I put more boundaries in my life?" Which is a socially acceptable way to say, "I might have codependency issues." Okay wait, I'm not saying *you* have codependency issues. We're talking about other women. Or sometimes clients will get a little more vulnerable and ask, "How do I find the one?" These questions are my jam.

I have a particular love for women struggling in and out of relationships. It's the reason I trained as a marriage and family therapist. I want to help women (read: myself) who are flubbing up relationships all over the place. Love is hard because it involves other people. And people, if you haven't noticed, are messy. They have all kinds of needs and quirks and don't seem to get at all how they impact others as they move about the cabin.

Relationships are also tricky because they are necessities. No matter how problematic they become, we can't just cut them out of our lives entirely. People are wired for human connection. Remember that verse about it not being good for man to be alone and all that jazz?[4] We need relationships like we need food—on the regular. Which is why working through a dysfunctional relationship is as hard as trying to beat an eating disorder. You can't just avoid the problem. Every few hours you have to bump up against your appetite for the very thing that's causing conflict.

But here's where I get concerned about the role relationships play in our search for meaning. It can be easy to define ourselves by our relational connections—so much so that we lose ourselves or devalue our individual worth outside of a relationship. Women, in particular, are vulnerable to this risk, especially when it comes to romance. Even with all our feminism and cultural progress, we still tend to encourage women to make securing a spouse the ultimate pursuit. Don't believe me? Ask any woman who has hit her midthirties and had to be a bridesmaid while single. She will affirm this. Catch her just after the bouquet toss, and she'll tell you how even if she has the dream job, owns her own home, and has a vibrant faith life, the other guests will still grab her to say, "That's great, honey. Why aren't you married? Let me introduce you to . . ." Girl, I see you. I'm sorry for their insensitivity. As they say in the South, bless their hearts.

My love for single women started during my early years in New York, when my best friend and I launched a Christian dating website called I Kissed Dating Hello. Yes, it was a riff on *I Kissed Dating Goodbye* by Joshua Harris. Yes, I went to Bible college. And yes, the site was awesome, so you're welcome.

As we talked about dating with young singles, we discovered

an interesting trend. Women, more so than men, kept putting their lives on hold in order to find "the guy." They would hold off on all kinds of big life moves they felt called to make for the possibility of a future relationship. Women would say things like "Well, I can't move out of the city even though that job looks great because what if my future husband is here and I leave?" Or "I think I want to start an organization in Uganda to help local women develop a microeconomy, but if I do that, how will I ever find a husband?" I'm sorry, wait, what?

On the flip side, when I would speak to women *in* relationships, the same thread was being pulled from the other side. Women would tell me all about the career moves their partners were making or the grand plans they had for how to spend the summer backpacking through Denmark. And I'd ask, "So is that your purpose or his? Is that what *you* feel called to do, or is that *his* life vision?" Often the woman had become so enmeshed with what her partner wanted that she couldn't tell the difference. She didn't know where he ended and she began. I could see women shrinking right before my eyes, turning into extras in the lives of their leading men.

In both cases, women were viewing their self-worth through the lens of the relationships they'd built. So let me say this loud for the women in the back in case you don't hear me. *Your singleness is not problematic.* Your relationship status does not set the bounds of who you are. With or without a partner, you've been created with a purpose. There is no asterisk in the Bible near Jeremiah 29:11 where God says, "For I know the plans I have for you." Stop acting as though that line has fine print stating: "Purpose cannot be redeemed or combined with other offers unless partnered." You matter, with or without anyone else.

However, women don't just do this with romantic relationships. It happens all over the place. Mothers lose themselves to caring for their children. Sisters get caught up in caring for siblings. Daughters wrestle with how to step into who they want to become and how to follow the family script. Women are taught to give up agency and allow the needs, expectations, and desires of others to inform how they behave. We're applauded for self-sacrifice. And Hallmark makes a killing each year on cards encouraging this behavior.

In case you're wondering, this kind of martyrdom doesn't work. At least not long term. Over time, I see the women suffocating from resentment or total loss of self. One of my favorite clients was a woman who successfully built a career working in the financial industry in New York City. No small feat in a ruthless male-dominated sector. Though she was thriving professionally, she was drowning personally.

When we worked together, I learned she had a passion for music she'd never explored. A talented songwriter, she had put her artistic dreams on hold because the rule in her family was "Be financially stable." So she studied business instead of music, choosing the safer path. Because she saw her life's worth primarily through the lens of who she loved (in this case, her family), she struggled to break out of the box they'd put her in. The more she accomplished, the more trapped she felt in a life she never would have chosen for herself. We had to work on getting her the courage to let go of being who they wanted so she could become who she was meant to be.

Do you have a robust vision for who you are outside of your relationships? When you think of your life purpose, do you immediately connect it to who you love or who you serve? Again, there is nothing wrong with making a significant contribution to the lives of others. However, you are more than your relationships.

LIMITING BELIEF #3: "I AM WHAT I HAVE"

Lastly, I see women living from the outside in by constructing their identity from stuff. Believing they are what they can acquire, they come to me fixated on getting more. Of course no one admits this at the outset. Few people lead with "Hi, I'm the sum of all the stuff I own. Nice to meet you." After all, we recognize the vanity in saying such things.

But as I speak with new clients and unearth their desires for the future, I see how gripped they are by the pressure to own more possessions. One woman described her proclivity to amass more things as an impulse to create a moat of security around her life so she never had to depend on anyone else for survival. Other clients talk as though life is a game they are losing—the winner being the one who finishes with all the spoils. I'll hear consumerism and materialism seep out in comments like "I haven't bought a home yet! Can you believe that? I have nothing to show for my life." One client told me, "I will know I have made it when I finally get the latest Tesla and pay for it in cash." Somewhere Elon Musk is smiling to himself and cashing a big check.

It's not always houses and cars though. Other women focus on smaller luxuries, like the desire to invest in new wardrobes or makeup regimens that suit their personal style. The form of consumerism I most enjoy helping my clients address? Travel. This one is sneaky because on the surface it sounds like a redemptive pursuit. "I'm cultured," they'll say. "I just want to explore the world and be adventurous. What's wrong with that?" Not much. It's just that in some cases, acquiring experiences is just like loading up mental shelves with memories the way hoarders fill a pantry. You want something outside of who you are.

Look, I'm not here to judge anyone. I want a white Range Rover with caramel leather interior just as much as the next Kardashian. But we need to acknowledge these are wants, not needs. Owning stuff does not equate to living a meaningful life. In *The Progress Paradox*, Gregg Easterbrook cautions, "The blurring of needs and wants is important here because needs can be satisfied . . . Wants, by contrast, can never be satisfied. The more you want, the more likely you are to feel disgruntled; the more you acquire, the more likely you are to feel controlled by your own possessions."[5] Oof. That cuts. We've been together for a couple chapters now, so let's be honest with one another. Do you feel controlled by your possessions or your desire for them? I sure do.

When I first moved to New York with two suitcases and a dream, I slept on the sofa of a friend of a friend for a month. I was the happiest I have ever been, even though I had a legitimate need for a room of my own. After working for a bit, I was able to pay for a space on the Upper East Side with two other twenty-somethings who'd just moved to the city. But once I landed that room for rent, a funny thing started to happen. I wanted a bigger room. And then I wanted an apartment for myself. And then I wanted a nicer apartment in a better neighborhood. Eventually my family and I left New York and bought a six-bedroom home in Georgia. Now I catch myself because there are moments when I still wish we had a little more. What if we had a playset in our backyard or a nicer deck or a pool or a . . . ? You get the idea. Wants don't tend to end.

Let's not be too hard on ourselves though. You and I didn't create the desire for a new iPad or a house in the 'burbs with a white picket fence. We've been internalizing this narrative of the good life since we were young. Think about it. When we talk about living the American Dream, what is the goal if not to be a good person who gets an education, lands a high-earning job, buys a home, finds a partner, vacations, maybe has children, and then dies? Isn't that what most of us have been taught to live for?

I say "taught" with magnanimity because the more accurate description is "preyed upon to believe." The entire goal of the advertising industry is to manufacture a sense of inadequacy so we internalize a longing to live a life that is not our own. We're taught to devalue what we have and fantasize about stuff we may not need. Never forget we're in a capitalist society where the American consumer spends on average $61,224 per year.[6] You'd better believe everyone wants a slice of that pie.

THE ROOT ISSUE

Which brings us back to the root issue and why I'm inviting you to live a courageously average life, shirking exceptionalism and outward success to become a woman of consequence. I want to encourage you to live for something that aligns more deeply with who you really are. What if instead of chasing significance by living from the outside in, you instead set your sights on becoming a woman of consequence? Let me outline the difference for you so you can pick your own path.

When I refer to women of *significance*, I'm talking about women whose self-definition is dependent on external markers of success. They have bought fully into the lie that their job, relationships, or possessions determine their worth. Therefore, women on the significance path spend their energy seeking something outside of themselves to soothe the ache of perceived inadequacy. As a result, a woman of significance often

- lacks self-awareness and doesn't know who she is or what she really wants;
- ignores her personal needs and desires to fulfill the needs and desires of others;
- derives her identity from her professional status;
- shape-shifts and conforms to everyone else;
- burns herself out working for the praise and affirmation of others.

On the other hand, women of *consequence* engage the world on a wildly different level. They are internally driven. These women accept that who they are is enough, and therefore what they do in the world is a product of their natural identity versus a means of producing their identity. As a result, a woman of consequence

- possesses a deep understanding of her individual wiring;
- commits to honoring her core needs and desires on a daily basis;
- lives holistically by growing in all life buckets;
- has the courage to be unlike anyone else;
- uses her gifts and talents joyfully to impact the world.

What kind of woman do you want to be?

I'm biased, but I hope you'll join me in choosing to be a

woman of consequence. I think it's the better path. I know our culture tells us to live bigger, louder, and faster than the person next to us by filling our lives with all the successes and spoils of the world, but I don't see that working out for most people. The women I know with the deepest joy and satisfaction are those who might be considered insignificant by the world's standards.

I think of women like my mother-in-law, Abigail Dokun, and my bonus mom, Monique Ruiz.† They'll never make headlines, but these are the women who have shown me what it means to *really* live. Their lives model healthy self-assuredness and contentment rooted in the belief that everything they are, do, and have is enough.

And maybe that's it in a nutshell. At the core of the desire for significance is the lie that you are not good enough right now, as you are. This lie severs the soul from reality.

I'm not trying to be dramatic. I think that's why women use language like "I don't know who I am" or "I feel like I'm missing out on my life." When we orient our lives fully in the direction of becoming something we are not, the only option is dissociation— disengaging from our everyday lives. It becomes harder and harder to live in our actual lives because we're so focused on becoming who we think we *should* be. We're cognitively living a different existence. I believe we need to relearn how to embody our own ordinary lives. When we embrace the ordinary, we begin to see the extraordinary nature of our daily existence.

So hear me on this: You are enough. You don't need to do, be,

---

† A quick word on my "bonus mom," Monique Ruiz. When I was sixteen years old, my life was forever changed by the woman I call "Mom #2." She generously gave me a home when my mother fell ill and could no longer take care of me. I owe much of my life's trajectory to the faithfulness of Monique, who listened to God's prompt to take in an angsty high schooler to love as her own child.

or acquire one more thing to make you significant. You simply need to live into who you already are. Maybe I'm showing my Bible college colors, but one of my favorite lines of scripture comes from Philippians 3:16. It says, "Let us live up to what we have already attained." How dope is that? You already have the life you're meant to live; you just need to live up to it. That's why I say the process of finding one's life purpose is truly about discovery, not creation. It's a hunt for who you were created to be, rather than trying to become something you are not.

Over the course of the next few chapters, we'll talk about how to begin unearthing who you are, not who you want to be. But before we go there, let's talk about why living an ordinary life takes courage. If we already know we're miserable in our current pursuit of the good life, why is it so hard to abandon the search for significance?

The answer is simple, and I blame Mark Zuckerberg, the Kardashians, and eharmony.

three

THE POWER OF YOUR DAILY LITURGIES

When the will and the imagination are in
opposition, the imagination always wins.

WENDY BACKLUND, *VICTORIOUS EMOTIONS*

Why is the search for significance so hard to shake?

Let's be real—this book isn't your first rodeo. My guess is
you've been striving to find ways to experience more meaning
within your life for years, and you have the receipts to prove it.
Maybe you, like me, are what Jefferson Bethke calls "informa-
tionally obese" because you have been "gorging [yourself] on
information" to optimize your life.[1] You've invested in countless
self-help books, downloaded all the sermons, and listened to all
the podcasts to recenter yourself on a regular basis. Am I right?
You already know you're meant to live from the inside out, rather
than striving for success and approval by becoming who the world
wants you to be. So what's the issue? Why aren't you doing it?

Okay, what's *my* issue? #helpasisterout

I have an idea. And it's one of those things that sounds complicated but is actually quite simple. So don't get scared off by the twenty-dollar words I'm about to throw at you. You know this stuff. I'm just going to apply some academic language to what you intuitively feel.*

So here goes: The problem we're facing is that our lives are driven by what we love, not by what we believe. We can't *think* our way into a life of consequence, because at its core, the search for significance is not a cognitive exercise. You can watch all of Oprah's *Super Soul Sunday* episodes, but you'll still be the same. More head knowledge will only go so far.

When it comes to how we live, the pursuit of the good life is *precognitive*, meaning it starts with a desire to experience a specific vision of human flourishing. That vision of the good life arrests our affections and begins to influence our actions. And these actions begin to make up a series of behaviors that, taken together, we call our lives.

Clear as mud, right?

Okay, let me break this down a little bit with the help of modern Christian philosopher James K. A. Smith.

THE POWER OF YOUR IMAGINATION

In his book *Desiring the Kingdom: Worship, Worldview and Cultural Formation*, Smith describes how people are *teleological*

---

* Okay, I should give you fair warning that I am about to nerd out on you over the next few pages. We're inching toward the intersection of my training in literature, theology, and psychology. So grab a cup of coffee because this is fascinating stuff. I want you to be free to live into the fullness of who you are. And you can't do that if you are trapped in an alternate reality. So—take the blue pill with me.

creatures. (There's that twenty-dollar word for you. Gird your loins.) What he means is, we don't solely exist in the world as a container of thoughts and ideas. Sure, we have beliefs. But our primary orientation to the world is intentional, not rational.

Consider it this way. You're not merely reading. You are reading this particular book. Furthermore, you're reading it because you have a desired outcome. Maybe you think reading this will help you figure out your life purpose. Maybe your friend recommended it and you want to read this book so you can talk to her about it later. Or maybe you simply think reading books like this makes you a more emotionally intelligent person. You're right about that last one, by the way.[2] So, we might say you're reading this book to demonstrate the kind of woman you want to be in the world. It's intentional.

Whether you are conscious of it or not, some ideal you have is driving your behavior. And this happens to you all day long in every area of your life. You move toward certain relationships, work a particular job, or add items to your online shopping cart based on the longings you have. These longings are the real riverbanks of your life, directing you toward a particular end, or *telos*, you have imagined.

So here's where this starts to get really interesting. Smith explained,

> Rather than being pushed by beliefs, we are pulled by a *telos* that we desire. It's not so much that we're intellectually convinced and then muster the willpower to pursue what we ought; rather at a precognitive level, we are attracted to a vision of the good life that has been painted for us in stories and myths, images and icons. It is not primarily our minds

that are captivated but rather our *imaginations* that are captured, and when our imagination is hooked, *we're* hooked (and sometimes our imaginations can be hooked by very different visions than what we're feeding into our minds).[3]

Oh snap.

THE DIFFERENCE BETWEEN HEART AND HEAD KNOWLEDGE

No wonder it's so hard to abandon the search for significance. Even when we know rationally that significance will not satisfy, if our imaginations have been swept up in fantasies of extraordinary lives, we are sunk. Our lives will organize themselves around the pursuit of what we envision. That's why it's easy to know intellectually that a mansion won't satisfy us, but we still spend our energy scrolling Zillow and trying to get that house on the hill anyway. It's heart over head, imagination over rationalization.

By the way, this is one of the reasons why advertising is a wildly effective, multibillion-dollar industry. Did you know the average American is exposed to between four thousand and ten thousand advertisements a day?[4] That's a lot of ads—about one every fifteen seconds. They pop up all over the place on television, our phones, digital tablets, books, magazines, and more. And many of these ads are introducing vivid commercial images to your mental catalog of the good life. Entire teams of advertising folks are working overtime to produce high-definition pictures and creative characters to capture your attention. Your focus is valuable, my friend. Advertisers know the truth of what Mary Oliver means when she wrote, "Attention is the beginning of devotion."[5] They know if they can grab you with quick, compelling story lines, they can woo your heart to desire a life that requires purchasing their particular good or service.

So pay attention to what has your attention. Do you routinely fantasize about your version of the good life and your purpose? Or are most of the mental images you have of the good life littered with other people's ideal lives? This isn't one of those rhetorical questions I want you to read and then gloss right over as you rush to the next paragraph. Let's pause for a moment. This is a good opportunity to uncover your default conceptualization of success. Think about it.

- What are some of the last television shows you watched?
- Which films have you seen recently?
- What was the last commercial you saw that made you laugh?
- Which magazines have you read lately?
- Whose social media feed do you tune in to most frequently?
- How were the heroes or most successful characters in each of these spaces depicted?
- When you envision "making it," who or what comes to mind?

And here I'm talking actual images. I want you to bypass your brain, moving beyond your espoused values and logic for what makes a good life. Trust that I view you at baseline as a modern-day Mother Teresa—so there's no need to try to impress me or lie to yourself with holier-than-thou posturing. Let's assume you have incredible character and remove judgment from the equation.

When you last saw someone thriving, what did it look like? Which images do you remember? Did any snapshots of success stick with you? We're interested in the pictures and plotlines of the good life that have gripped your heart.

If you're like me or most of my clients, you probably imagine a celebrity or something you saw on Netflix or *MTV Cribs* back in the day. When I asked one of my clients what she pictured, she mentioned a Justin Bieber documentary where he and his model wife, Hailey, were traveling on a private jet. She giggled at the retelling because she's not much of a Belieber—she got lost in a Hulu documentary search gone rogue. But the film left a strong impression on my client. In her mind she saw a beach vacation, the freedom of the horizon line, and unlimited resources to take her wherever she wanted to go at a moment's notice. She couldn't stop thinking about it.

My fantasies of the good life look like Joanna Gaines surrounded by shiplap in a modern farmhouse or Oprah road-tripping across America with Gayle. Sometimes I picture Kerry Washington as the character Olivia Pope from *Scandal*. In my mind's eye she's wearing one of those flawlessly tailored trench coats and a white hat as she storms into the Oval Office for a passionate (and illicit) embrace with President Fitz. Don't judge me. This is what pops into my imagination.

I've acquired these images from years of TV watching, and they are so vivid I can almost smell the chocolate chip cookies in Joanna's perfectly designed kitchen or hear Gayle and Oprah arguing over what song to play next on the radio.

And the more I picture it, the more I want it.

Or at least I feel like I do.

Maybe.

Not really.

Because if I start to walk myself back from these arche-types of the good life, I realize how in conflict they are with my talents, wiring, and values. Unlike Joanna, I have zero spatial intelligence, so redecorating a big home in Texas sounds like a frustrating exercise. Strike one. And while I love hanging out with friends occasionally, the ideal vacation for this introvert is a weekend alone by the beach reading a book. Strike two. And sorry, Shonda Rhimes[†]—I'm a married woman. There is nothing sexy to me about infidelity. I don't want to become the mistress to the president of the United States. Strike three, and I'm out. These images don't encourage a hunger for the life I am choosing consciously to live.

But here's the irony.

It's amazing how these powerful images and story lines have nestled into my subconscious. They stoke within me a longing for a life I don't even want. I wouldn't immediately admit this, but when I look at my daily actions, the proof is in the pud-ding. So much so that I find myself taking small actions more in line with the pursuit of these potential lives than the life I say I want. Cue me buying a Hearth & Hand dish towel at Target, made by Joanna Gaines. The next day I'm texting a friend with links to a spa in the Midwest that we "just have to visit one day." Another afternoon I'm wondering how to spice up my sex life

---

[†] Can we take a second to celebrate Shonda Rhimes? I love her work. Shonda is the incredible writer and creator of shows like *Grey's Anatomy*, *How to Get Away with Murder*, and *Bridgerton*. I'm always tuned in to see what she'll create next.

and searching the interwebs for new lingerie for a racy night with hubby.

And hey, there is nothing wrong with these actions . . . on occasion. I watch one episode of *Fixer Upper*; I see a beautiful towel I want, and I buy it. No big deal. Who is hurt in the process?

But what if this became more of a pattern? What if I watched the show every day? Joanna's vision of a beautiful lifestyle might become more deeply imprinted in my mind and heart for what it means to live on purpose. If I made a habit of watching the show, it might train me to desire what it depicts. And not only that, but the very routine of watching TV itself might be forming me into a certain kind of person.

OUR HIDDEN LITURGIES

Smith calls these types of habits—like binge-watching home renovation shows—*liturgies* because they serve as formative practices in our lives.‡ Liturgies also have a reciprocal effect with our desires.

We develop habits based on our longings. That's obvious; we act according to our desires. But the process also works in reverse. Our liturgies can create longings within us, reinforcing certain ideals about what is to be desired in the world. Now that's

---

‡ By the way, I'm a big fan of using the term *liturgies* instead of *habits*. Call me Demi Lovato because "sorry not sorry." The term landed in my lap back in 2010 after James K. A. Smith spoke to my church in New York. It was like the veil falling. His use of the word *liturgy* to speak of ordinary rituals—stuff like checking email, riding the subway, and shopping for groceries—cast a holy filter across all of my activities and broke through the sacred and secular division that characterized my lifestyle. I hope this language helps you also see that the ordinariness of your daily life is forming you into a certain kind of person. May it invite you to consider who you are becoming.

a different angle altogether that we need to take note of as women of consequence. We don't just do what we want; we want what we do. The liturgies of our lives tell our hearts what to love.

Here's where the scales started to fall from my eyes, and I hope this will feel like a helpful insight for you, too, as you analyze your own life purpose journey: That false self you've constructed through the years, the one that's leaving you suffocated and drowning, is likely the product of good but not great liturgies you're practicing again and again.

You're not crazy. Put that on a Post-it and stick it on your bathroom mirror. It's not surprising that you feel caught unaware of the predicament you're in now with a "good but not great" life you don't fully love. You're not drowning because you leapt into the deep end and attempted to live into a life that was wildly outside of who you are. You've just been innocently splashing around over here in the kiddie pool, doing your thing day after day, and slowly you got disoriented by the liturgies of your life. The seemingly innocuous rituals you engage in each day have been training your heart and directing your life toward an end you may not logically want to pursue.

At least that's what happened to me. When I made the move from Los Angeles to New York City after college, I was driven by a longing to realize a very specific version of the good life I imagined. My heart had been captured by the idea of working in publishing for a big New York magazine and making connections in the hip-hop and spoken word circles that filled small clubs all around the city. I should mention that while I had some background in writing, the hip-hop scene was not at all my world. I was the girl obsessed with Justin Timberlake, not Kanye West. But one liturgy of my life post-college wooed my heart to desire a lifestyle I didn't really want. The film *Dave Chappelle's Block Party* had just come out, which starred the comedian and a bunch of musicians like Erykah Badu, the Roots, and Mos Def as they held an outdoor concert in the Clinton Hill neighborhood of Brooklyn. I watched the movie almost every day, mesmerized by the picture of New York the film depicted. I wanted that life. Being a creative and living in Brooklyn seemed like the most glorious future I could imagine.

Set on becoming a New Yorker, I started to disengage from my life in LA. *NSYNC albums were swapped out for records by the Fugees. I traded green smoothies for bagels and schmear at breakfast. I was no longer interested in the church community I'd grown in Hollywood or the friendships I'd built with alumni from my school in the surrounding area. I was enraptured by neo soul music, the gritty life of Brooklyn, and the intersection of spoken word poetry and comedy. Months later I dropped everything in California and moved, with two suitcases, to New York, where I eventually landed an apartment just six blocks from where the Dave Chappelle movie was filmed.

That's the power of a little liturgy.

I want to help you notice the desire-forming liturgies in your life so you can discern for yourself what is helpful or harmful to your individual thriving. Our goal is for you to start living your version of the good life now, free and unhindered by practices that keep you tethered to a life you don't want. The process of reclaiming your life starts with reclaiming your longings.

Let me share what this looks like for some of my clients as we've illuminated the connections between their hidden life liturgies and derailed life direction through the years.

Rachel: An iPhone Love Affair

"I'm addicted to my phone," Rachel confessed. "I carry it everywhere I go—even the bathroom. Is that gross?" Rachel, thirty-six, was a typical smartphone user. She had the latest iPhone and spent hours on it texting friends, sending work emails, and scrolling social media. When I told Rachel that a 2019 study said the average American checks their phone ninety-six times a day (about once every five to ten minutes during waking hours), she thought that number sounded low. Her screen time reports showed she was on her phone for hours, and like most people, she spent at least two and a half hours a day on apps like Instagram and Facebook alone.[6] For Rachel, checking her phone had become a liturgy.

As we began to unpack her habit, we looked at how constantly checking her phone influenced her life. First, the social media scrolling had the obvious impact of skewing her vision of the good life. Her feed was full of friends on vacation, couples smooching, entrepreneurs in carefully curated work-from-anywhere scenes, and more. Even though she knew these filtered images were faux highlight reels, with all the yucky parts of life edited out to put up a good front, they still served as a running slideshow for her imagination of the good life. She admitted, "I know it's not real, but it feels like everyone else is living a fabulous life. Meanwhile, I'm sitting here with my pants around my ankles in the bathroom, swiping through their extraordinary moments."

We also noticed how, outside of the content she was ingesting from social media, the very act of checking her phone was shifting Rachel's interaction with her ordinary life. Every time she started to focus and dig into her own experience, she paused, set her real life aside, and unlocked her phone to check Twitter or Instagram. The message she was sending herself was clear: The real action was online. If Rachel ever wanted to embrace the joy of her ordinary life, we needed to help her put the phone down and intentionally tell herself a new story of her own value.

Camille: A Mom Trying to Measure Up to the Kardashians

Camille, thirty-eight, was a single mom drowning in credit card debt. She spent a lot of money buying her daughter toys or paying for experiences she couldn't afford. She was exhausted from trying to balance working full-time with full-time motherhood. She'd come to me wanting to "be a better mom," so I asked Camille to describe what excellence looks like in parenting. She said the perfect mom is someone who provides for her child, gives unconditional love, and is present. I asked if she did those things, and she responded, "Well, I'm no Kris Jenner, but yes, I do. I just wish I could give my daughter more. I don't know where this ache is coming from, but I always feel like I'm not measuring up."

Her anxiety around parenting didn't logically follow. Plus, I couldn't ignore the Kris Jenner reference. We needed to get out of her head and drop into the heart space. So I asked Camille to share what images she held of motherhood and to tell me about the last moms she'd seen on TV. She laughed and said she was a total reality TV junkie, so it was probably the Kardashians or Kylie Jenner. Every night after her daughter went to bed, she numbed out with a couple episodes of *Keeping Up with the Kardashians*. She loved watching the latest drama between the sisters and was "obsessed" with the glitz and glamour of their home life. She knew the situations were manufactured and almost nothing about the shows were "real," but she couldn't get enough.

I eyed the red bottoms of her heels as she pulled out her Kylie Cosmetics lip kit, and when our eyes met again, it was like we both made the connection at the same time. She was subconsciously trying to become a reality TV mom. We worked on unraveling her concept of motherhood by cutting down her TV time and creating a vision board with photos of moms doing the things she valued each day.

Jada: Swiping Right into a Life She Didn't Want

Jada really wanted to get married. After years of trying to meet someone through personal connections, she decided to give online dating a try. She signed up for eharmony and within a couple weeks started to see a steady stream of matches landing in her inbox. The whole platform felt a little awkward to her. She wasn't sure what to say or how to assess the men she was being matched with each week. So she developed a habit of sharing the profile of each guy she encountered with a friend. They'd talk through the match, dissecting every word, spelling error, and preference he had until she could eliminate that particular guy as an option. Jada usually found a flaw and quickly moved on to the next guy, trusting someone better would always come along. She rarely went on actual dates.

When I met with Jada, she was frustrated by her dating experience and ready to throw in the towel. She complained that no one was good enough and wondered aloud if she was asking too much. I affirmed that online dating was indeed difficult. Relationship expectations have radically shifted in the past couple decades, so it wasn't all in her head. However, I wondered if something about the way she engaged in online dating was negatively impacting her results. It sounded to me like she approached the process looking for flaws, and her time spent debriefing potential dates with a friend sounded a lot like the way someone might shop for a new outfit that suits them. *Does this match make my butt look big?* I suspected she'd lost her humanity.

The liturgy she had created around online dating made the process more similar to online shopping than building a relationship. She was acting like a customer and expecting each guy to wow her and be worth her time. That kind of self-centered focus isn't at all the posture needed to establish a relationship. We needed to work on how she could re-engage in online dating with a relationship-oriented mindset.

Okay, let's pause for a second. Because about now is the moment when you start getting suspicious of me. You might be thinking, *Who is this woman? What's her agenda?* And you're concerned you've been duped or accidentally stepped into the world of a conspiracy theory–peddling killjoy with an ax to grind against cell phone developers, reality TV, and all online dating platforms.

Don't worry. The only thing I hate about Apple is the fact that they changed the ports on my laptop, so I can't use my old charger. And I'm pro online dating! I met my husband on eharmony, so I'm one of those crazy people who believes it's possible to find lasting love through dating apps. If you want to use your iPhone to swipe right on some guy you found on Bumble who seems like a good candidate to bring home to Mama, do you, boo. I'm also not going to tell you to cancel your Netflix subscription or delete your Instagram account[§] because the Kardashians and Mark Zuckerberg are out to get you. No need to ring the alarm.

Let me be clear. You're an adult. You get to choose how you're going to live your own life. But I want you to begin to increase your awareness of the impact that these types of cultural goods have on you and your ability to pursue the life you want. Remember, you're drowning. I'm trying to help you get your bearings. You deserve to know which way is up so you're not caught with your booty aimed high to the sky in the middle of a *Schitt's Creek* marathon. You have to start to see yourself as separate from the water. Be in it and not of it, if you know what I mean. This is one of the first steps in getting your head above water.

You start by coming to accept that your daily habits are not neutral. Your life liturgies are forming you into a particular kind of woman and pulling you in all sorts of directions. That's why you might feel out of alignment. If you don't like the life you have now, start evaluating what you're doing that is reinforcing the life you don't want. I want to empower you to decide if the liturgies of your life are redemptive or destructive. Redemptive liturgies remind us who we are. They invite us back to ourselves and allow us to grow a desire for the life we're meant to live. Destructive liturgies are those that pull us away from the women we want to be. They draw us into an alternate reality and hard-wire our hearts to love the very version of the good life we despise.

Rather than give you a good/bad list of liturgies—as if I could ever tell you what serves you best—I want to give you my one-word filter for assessing your life rhythms. I've already mentioned it briefly because I'm sneaky like that. I'm a mind ninja

§ You can follow me on Instagram @chanel.dokun. Let's be #instafriends and get to know way too much about each other's lives.

with no chill. I want to help you hurry into the life you're meant to live, so it's hard to hold back all I want to share with you. The gate I use to filter liturgies is *dissociation*.

In the next chapter, let's define dissociation, explore what it means to experience it, and discuss how watching for liturgies that cause dissociation in your life can radically help you get back to yourself. I'll help you see through the matrix and give you the number one practice I recommend for clients so you can develop the courage required to live out your own redemptive, purpose-driven liturgies.

Ready? Let's go.

four

THE COURAGE TO
BE NOBODY

Make it your ambition to lead a quiet life: You should
mind your own business and work with your hands.

1 THESSALONIANS 4:11

Believe it or not, we've already covered a lot of ground. Maybe it feels like we've just been chatting. But I've been not-so-secretly inching you along to begin confronting the big concepts that will help you know which way is up in your life so you can get your head above water.

Let's recap.

We've established that the life you're living now is not the life you want. Simply powering through and trying harder is problematic because it keeps you on a hamster wheel, chasing a life of significance that can never satisfy. And we've acknowledged that if you're ever going to stop drowning in shallow water, you need to let go of your search for significance and move from external identity formation to internal formation.

That means creating the unique life God means for you to live. But . . .

This process is tough as nails because it's not an *intellectual* reframe. Rather, a habitual shift is required along with the mindset change to remold your heart to long for the kind of life that would ultimately be fulfilling for you. I can't emphasize this enough. I've helped lots of women discover their life purpose. But insight alone doesn't lead to change in their lives. The women who experience transformation are those who make tangible changes to their daily rhythms to reflect the insight they've gained. That means first identifying the destructive liturgies, or regular routines, forming your life in the way of seeking external significance.

Whoa. Give yourself a slow clap for attentiveness.

Here's where things start to get a little active. We want to begin rooting out purpose-draining practices so you can be unhindered to discover the fullness of your life purpose. Right now your daily practices may be encouraging you to devalue the ordinary life you're living. Once you're armed with a sense of direction, you can then proactively integrate supportive life rhythms that help you desire and lean into the life you want. Our goal for you is lasting change.

I say this like it's easy.

It's not easy.

But don't worry. I'm going to walk you through it step-by-step.

In the next few chapters, I'm going to give you practical tools you can use to discover your life purpose. I'll break down the anatomy of a strong life mission statement so you can have a custom guiding mantra to direct your steps. And I'll help you get back into your own skin by amplifying your identity through a three-step process. I'll show you how to put language to your talents, honor your heart, and best steward the influence God has given you.

In the last chapter, I told you I'd show you how to evaluate the liturgies of your life so you can remove those that are destructive and amplify the habits that move you closer to your life purpose. For me, the beginning with clients is always a life assessment—because we can't treat what we haven't diagnosed, and we can't diagnose what we haven't assessed.

So what does that look like? When I provide a life assessment for my clients, I ask them to share with me the basic details of their lives. What do they do for work? How do they spend their free time? Who do they see on a regular basis? What personal habits do they keep or never have enough time for? All the good stuff. I fill pages upon pages with notes about who they are so I can later reflect back to them much of what I've heard. While they're providing a brief inventory, I'm listening for a host of information that will be useful in our work together as we figure out their life purpose.

But the one bit of information I'm listening for and rarely communicate is my assessment of their life liturgies. I'm sifting through their routines for sources of life support. I want to know how much of their time is spent on redemptive, purpose-affirming liturgies that help them grow more into who they are, and how much energy is going to destructive, life-draining liturgies that cause confusion and a crisis of identity. My dear friend Rasheeda Winfield calls this identifying the place where you're pouring your TEA—meaning where you are pouring your time, energy, and attention.[*]

---

[*] I'm hugely indebted to Rasheeda Winfield. Aside from holding my hand through writing this book via Marco Polo videos, she's a phenomenal producer and a woman you should follow online.

As I'm listening, I categorize their activities based on their level of dissociation. And it's this framework I want to share with you as you learn to evaluate how the habits in your life are wooing you to love a life of consequence or a life of significance. Most liturgies are subjective in their impact. No one habit affects all of us the same way. Based on how we're each wired, we can engage in the same habits but take from them a wildly different meaning.

For example, for one woman, an elaborate morning routine that includes making pour-over coffee might indicate slowing down to pay attention to her senses as she smells the ground beans and watches the caramel-colored liquid drip into her cup (redemptive). For another, the same routine could mean trying to replicate what she saw an influencer do on Instagram, and it's a daily reinforcement to put on an identity that's not her own (destructive). Do you see how subjective liturgies can be? Given this, I can't create arbitrary metrics for you based on things like money or even time spent to guide you on what is helpful or harmful to the development of your purpose. But the impact of *dissociative liturgies* is always clear.

WHAT IS DISSOCIATION?

Dissociative liturgies are those repetitive activities that train us to cognitively live outside of our actual lives. They take us away from being present. When we look back at this period of time, I believe one of the greatest tragedies we'll find is the hidden epidemic of normalizing dissociation. That's a fancy way of saying our cultural rhythms train people to regularly check out of their lives, to interact with one another in a manufactured hyperreality. We'll talk more about this, but first let's define what dissociation is so you don't keep getting tripped up on that term. Let's have the same working connotation.

Dissociation is really about disconnection and separation. It's that out-of-body feeling when you lose track of time and space. It might give you the heebie-jeebies.[†] In psychology, we tend to talk about dissociation as related to extreme cases, like dissociative identity disorder, where someone feels like their identity splits into two or more distinct personalities. It's also a common response to trauma, so those of us who work predominantly with women frequently encounter clients who use dissociation as a coping mechanism. Half of all women will experience a traumatic event in their lifetime, and women are twice as likely as men to experience PTSD.[1] In light of this, dissociation is par for the course.

But in a nonpathological sense, it's not unusual for all of us to experience mild, momentary dissociation throughout our lives. Especially in times of stress or distraction, we might feel disconnected from ourselves. In these cases, dissociation shows up as feeling separated from your own mental processes (like operating on autopilot), identity confusion (an existential crisis), or derealization ("I don't even recognize where I am right now").

Short instances of dissociation are fine. You mentally check out for a second while you're driving down the highway and a Lizzo song comes on the radio.[‡] Suddenly you're imagining yourself playing the flute onstage at the Grammys while a celebrity-filled audience cheers for you. No problem. Muscle

---

† I'm pretty sure that's a technical term, by the way, but I'm not confident. *Siri, remind me to google "heebie-jeebies" later.*

‡ I first heard Lizzo's song "Truth Hurts" in the movie *Someone Great* with Gina Rodriguez. I was obsessed. I consider it a personal achievement that I managed to integrate this into my first book, and I will ask my husband to add to my tombstone, "Here lies Chanel, who always found a way to make a Lizzo reference."

memory allows you to keep the car moving while your brain continues to process your eyes' signals about what's ahead of you. It lasts a moment, and you hop right back into yourself before you rear-end another car. No harm done.

But what if this became a habit? You can imagine how problematic dissociation might be if it lasted longer than a few seconds on a long drive. If you repeatedly thought you were Lizzo and then started to interact with others *as* her, we might wonder if you were insane. Or what if your life choices started to be based more on what Lizzo needed than what was best for you? You might spend a lot of money or time on things that have no value to you, such as personal security guards or expensive concert flutes. Soon your real life might be neglected while your TEA is being poured into upholding a fantasy of another life.

When reality finally hits, you might show up in my office saying, "Chanel, I have all these things in my life that are great, but they don't feel meaningful. I'm wearing clothes that don't fit, buying instruments I can't play, and my relationships feel weird and distant. Something is off balance. I think I need help recovering my authentic self beneath the veneer of someone else's life." Sound like something you might say even now?

That's kind of what's happening to us on a daily basis. We've made it a habit to inhabit other lives. And it's killing us. In *The Body Keeps the Score*, psychiatrist Bessel A. van der Kolk called on mental health practitioners to, above all else, help clients "live fully and securely in the present." Breaking the habit of dissociation and desensitization is critical because the stakes are high. He wrote, "If you cannot feel satisfaction in ordinary everyday things like taking a walk, cooking a meal, or playing with your kids, life will pass you by."[2]

Through our technology, entertainment, and other modern rhythms, we are routinely transported to either an idealized version of our own life or swept up in the current of other people's lives. And this habit makes it harder and harder to pay attention to our core self because we're constantly moving further away from who we are, what we need, and who we love.

I'm using the language of habit intentionally. Dissociation isn't problematic as a fleeting thought process or belief. It's disruptive in its cumulative effect. When it shows up repeatedly in the actions we take, it starts to form how we engage with the world around us. It becomes a destructive liturgy.

In the last chapter, I shared with you some of the liturgies of my past clients. Remember Rachel, who couldn't put down her iPhone? She's a great example of a woman gripped by dissociation. Rachel wanted to optimize her life. But she so rarely spent time in it. Most of her energy went to branding herself online as she retooled her social media presence and obsessed over how she was being perceived by others in her posts. She rarely posted the version of Rachel people experienced in real life. Online she added a filter or included a clever remark in the caption (one she never really said) to best represent how she hoped others would view her. There was the real Rachel and then the brand of Rachel. Slowly that divide started to take over, to the point where she could barely reconcile the two images.§

---

§ By the way, when did it become normal to start branding ourselves? Maybe I'm telling my age, but I remember when people lived their lives without giving much thought to their personal brand. Sure, style in some form has always existed. But the strategic manufacturing of self as brand is staggering to me. Something tells me we're not meant to be commodified for the consumption of others. And yet here we are, daily putting ourselves into these little boxes like packaged goods to be placed on digital shelves for one another. I don't know. Call me crazy, but I think you're more complex than a box of Kraft Macaroni & Cheese.

When she wasn't figuring out how to show up on social media, Rachel was lost in an internet hole, following the bunny trail of articles online. Instead of her screen time leading her to think more about her own life or to connect with people she knew and cared about, it caused her to dissociate. She would unlock her phone and be transported to a world of celebrity gossip, news on world events she could do nothing about, podcast episodes on more topics than any one person could possibly care about, and more. She was cramming in the cares of a life that was not her own with little room to think her own thoughts.

Do you know anyone like Rachel? I sure do. I know about thirty women like her, and to be honest, I'm often Rachel. I'm part of the league of women dissociating from life through a handheld device that's supposed to make things easier. But it doesn't make my life easier. It makes my life more confusing and noisy, to the point where I often can't hear my own voice above the pings of notifications.

And if we want to be formed from the inside out, instead of by the machinations of other people, we need to be able to hear ourselves. Our internal voice and the voice of God need to be loudest among the chorus of proclamations for how to live the good life. Because if they're not, their tone might become indiscernible to us in the moments it matters most.

This is why dissociation is so problematic and sneaky in its impact. Liturgies that cause us to disconnect from ourselves and our actual lives dull our ability to recognize ourselves when we *do* show up. They reduce the confidence we need to have in ourselves to pursue a life that would be meaningful in our estimation.

Here's a question. Have you ever felt at a loss when it comes to describing what you are passionate about? If I asked you to give me a list of twenty-five things you love to do right now, would you be able to rattle off your list in less than five minutes? Or would you feel stumped after about four or five things and start to have a mini panic attack? If quickly identifying what you love feels like a struggle, it might be a clue that your life has become too noisy. Dissociation has snuck in where you're taking up less space in your own life, and other voices are filling the void.

I know right now it feels like we're talking about a silly habit of doom-scrolling social media or checking your phone throughout the day. So let me fast-forward to the future so you can see how this can sabotage your ability to live into your purpose long term. Because I want you to see the compound effect of these actions. I recently worked with a client who had adopted a liturgy of daydreaming. Here's how that dissociative habit started to play out in her life.

Penelope: "I Daydream a Lot"

Penelope came to me hoping to discover her purpose. She talked about how she had a very hard time knowing herself and was constantly looking for reassurance from other people to confirm that the things she believed about herself were true. I was struck by her distrust of her own self-conceptualization. When we developed her list of talents (something I'll help you do in chapters 7 and 8), she was less interested in how she saw herself and more invested in my opinion of her. When it came time to write her life purpose statement, she pulled out a first draft a friend had written for her rather than starting with her own. Turn after turn, I watched her shirking responsibility for her own life. Long before we met, she'd stopped listening to herself, so when we connected, she was deeply embedded in a habit of elevating other people's opinions over her own. This made it hard for her to wade out of the shallow water.

Throughout our time working together, Penelope repeatedly expressed discontent about various areas of her life. But when I'd try to honor her dissatisfaction by drilling down into a particular topic to uncover what was wrong, it was clear there was no legitimate issue. For example, Penelope complained of not having community but would follow her complaint with descriptions of weekly hangouts and intimate prayer meetings she had with groups of friends. When I suggested maybe it was the quality of the friendships and not the quantity we needed to enhance, she dismissed it by saying she had more than a few solid relationships with people she could connect with on a deep level. If anything, she felt *too* busy and needed time away from people.

I was confused. Did she need community or not? What was the problem? Her reactions didn't seem to follow from what was sitting in front of me—which made it clear to me that some level of dissociation was driving her life, because I felt like I was dealing with two different people. Whenever a problem is too difficult to define, it usually means we're too distant from the components. We needed to get her back into her body.

At one point she paused and admitted, "I spend a lot of time fantasizing. I'm always living out different story lines in my head. I have a really active imagination."

Bingo. That was the problem.

Penelope had developed a habit of mentally ejecting herself from her real life. She'd picked up the habit as a kid to cope with the traumatic environment in which she lived. When her mom and dad fought, mentally she would hop on the back of a prince's horse to ride away from the terror. Now, as an adult, she couldn't shake the habit even when she was safe. As a result, when she assessed how she was doing, she had a hard time keeping tabs on which version of herself she was measuring. The imaginary version of her felt more real than the real her.

We needed to get her back into her own body before she could begin to live out her life plan. I recommended she start therapy to unpack some of the trauma in her life that had prompted her to dissociate. In her case, we needed to break through more than just a habit of checking her phone too much or making a small shift in her routine. Daydreaming was a coping mechanism she developed as a child, but it was now keeping her from embracing the very good life she was living as an adult. Grieving her lost childhood and learning mindfulness skills were the solutions she needed before she could begin embracing her life purpose.

THE POWER OF BEING PRESENT

I'll say it again. It's not just Penelope or Rachel. We all have something in our lives that is likely carrying us away from ourselves on a regular basis. What is it for you? What habits have you built up that take you out of your life story? Remember, momentary escapes are fine. We all need to relax and watch some Netflix from time to time. (Can I get an amen?) There is no shame in taking a break from the regular rhythms of life. But we're talking about more than a short escape.

What kinds of activities fill your schedule and keep you living just outside the bounds of who you are? What do you do that invites you into someone else's narrative of life, so much so that you can easily forget your own? We need to name and release these liturgies to get you back into your own body, heart, and mind so you can live a life of consequence.

But how?

If you've learned to cope by leaving your body, how do you retrain yourself to sit in your own skin? You have to start by believing that what got you here won't get you there, as the saying goes. The tools that worked in one phase of life might actually be an impediment for this new phase.

My recommendation for Penelope was to get back into therapy. Psychotherapy is a great option; everyone can benefit from talking to a therapist at some point in their lives. I'm not just saying that because I own a therapy practice.⁵ I say it as a patient, not as a practitioner. We can all benefit from Jesus *and* therapy. I want to remove the stigma from upping your mental health game.

It's a power move when you decide to prioritize getting psychological and emotional coaching to operate at your highest level. Think of it like this. Serena Williams doesn't have a tennis coach because she's bad at tennis. She has a coach because she wants to keep getting better. Be like Serena. Be better—by any means necessary. If you feel stuck in dysfunctional patterns or you've never invested in working with an expert to guide you toward greater mental health, what are you waiting for?

Beyond therapy, I think most of us can benefit from the underlying objective I was hoping Penelope would achieve with a little support. I wanted her to stop retreating from her life. That's something you can start doing now on your own, and in the next

---

§ FYI: My husband, Dr. Lanre Dokun, and I cofounded a therapy practice in New York City called Healthy Minds NYC. We are essentially the Beyoncé and Jay-Z of mental health. He hates when I say that. I'm stubborn and don't care. We'll work it out in couples therapy.

chapter I'll give you a tool so you're equipped before we head into figuring out your life purpose. We can all benefit from developing a simple mindfulness practice that encourages us to sit in our own skin and be present.

THE PRACTICE OF MINDFULNESS

By the way, I'm not the only one advocating for mindfulness. Have you noticed the uptick in apps and programs to help carve out time to be present? Don't write this off as woo-woo expansiveness or secular self-transcendence. I suspect the reason mindfulness has become so pervasive is because our culture has caught on that we need a solution to combat the epidemic of dissociation. From Headspace to Shine to Soulspace, an abundance of tools exist now to slow you down so you can focus on the moment. Don't even get me started on the number of books saturating the market. I did an online search for anything with *mindfulness* in its title, and I got thirty thousand book results . . . from just the past ninety days! I'm saying we've got options.

And while I have read more than my fair share of books on mindfulness, my favorite guru is my son. He's five years old and knows how to be alive to the moment better than anyone I know. Recently, our family went on a road trip from Georgia down to the panhandle in Florida. I'm an Enneagram one, also known as "The Perfectionist," who always needs the ideal plan for absolutely everything. So as we prepared for the trip, I started getting anxious about how to entertain my son on the five-hour drive. I called in the "text thread troops," asking all my mommy friends for ideas on how to manage the time in the car. Based on their suggestions, I loaded up our SUV with a whole bunch of games and sticker books, snacks galore, and his trusty iPad. I was ready.

And you know what happened? He ended up taking a short nap at the start of the drive. Then he ate lunch and ultimately stared out the window for three hours. I repeat, my five-year-old stared out the window for three hours! Occasionally he would direct comments to us up front like "Mommy, did you see that cloud? It looked like a bear." Then twenty minutes later he'd remark, "Wow, we're going fast. Can you feel the car moving? It's like a race car." At five years old, he mastered the ability to be present in his own body. I wanted to anesthetize him to the discomfort of the journey by entertaining him away from the reality of the long drive until we could get to "vacation." But he knew the real vacation started the moment we pulled out of the driveway. The fun was in being who he was right then in the moment without all the props.

THE COURAGE TO BE NOBODY

This kind of present living takes courage. On the one hand, it's simple enough for a five-year-old to do, but on the other, it can be frightening. Showing up to life empty-handed and without a game plan is risky. At least for a time.

I mean, don't get me wrong—I'm captain of #TeamPlan. As a professional life planner by trade, I value having a blueprint. In fact, I'm going to spend the remainder of this book helping you make one for your life. But the first stop on the road back to you is sitting uncomfortably in your own identity without anything to distract or affirm you. It's creating a space where you suspend all the destructive liturgies that cause you to dissociate and allow yourself to tap into your own voice.

And this is terrifying, to be honest. To momentarily release everything you've come to define as meaningful in life and be a nobody, arms suspended in the air without a clear identity—that takes bravery. It would be far easier to live a life of significance shaped by someone else. That road is already marked out for you. It's the well-trod path most people are taking, but "broad is the road that leads to destruction."[3] Are you willing to choose the narrower path?

I'll tell you how I first stumbled upon the necessity for nobody-ness. In college I studied twentieth-century American literature, and one of my favorite authors was J. D. Salinger.** You might be familiar with his most popular book on teenage angst, *The Catcher in the Rye*. But one of his works I love most is called *Franny and Zooey*, a short novel that originally appeared in the *New Yorker* about two siblings navigating spirituality and the emotional strains of entering adulthood. In it Salinger tucked a line that leapt from the page and grabbed me by the throat when I was in my late twenties trying to make something of myself in New York City.

Frustrated by ego and the cultural pressure to perform, Franny tells her boyfriend, Lane, "Just because I'm so horribly conditioned to accept everybody else's values, and just because I like applause and people to rave about me, doesn't make it right. I'm ashamed of it. I'm sick of it. I'm sick of not having the courage to be an absolute nobody. I'm sick of myself and everybody else that wants to make some kind of a splash."[4]

** When I say "favorite authors," I mean my best friends and I started the Salinger Sisters Book Club. My only regret is we never made T-shirts.

How gripping is that? When I read that line, it shook my soul because I thought, *That's the problem. That's the reason I'm drowning. My whole life is oriented around trying to become somebody, and I am exhausted by the effort.* Much like Franny, I longed to stop performing and trying to be who I thought I needed to be for my life to have significance. I needed courage to be comfortable being me.

What about you? Do you have the courage to be an absolute nobody? Are you sick of trying to win the applause of others and internalizing the values and expectations set before you? Or are you ready to give up the charade and really start pursuing a life worth living? It may be a Salinger line, but I suspect it's the way of the gospel. The kingdom of God runs on a currency of paradox: "Whoever finds their life will lose it, and whoever loses their life for my sake will find it."[5]

Are you ready to lose your life? That stuffy, ill-fitting, and suffocating life that is sapping your soul of the vibrant life you were promised? In the next chapter, I'll show you how so you can reclaim control over your life story. It starts with a simple practice you can do every morning before you even finish your cup of coffee.

Grab a notebook and meet me in the next chapter as I teach you how to reclaim the morning.

five

HOW TO RECLAIM
THE MORNING

I'm reclaiming my time.

REPRESENTATIVE MAXINE WATERS

I should preface this chapter by confessing that I'm not a morning person. It's critical you understand this about me, because in the health and wellness space there are a flock of experts who like to talk about miraculous mornings where they spend anywhere from two to twelve delightful hours doing God knows what before seven a.m. They will regale you with tales of how HIIT exercises, cacao turmeric lattes, and Post-it affirmations can unlock the secret to your success, if only you would adopt their methods.

These experts are almost always (you guessed it) male. Or at least privileged individuals who don't have to contend with putting on magnetic lashes or cleaning up diaper blowouts before caffeine hits their bloodstream. As a result, these ~~serial killers~~

morning people pop out of bed, rosy and bright, rejoicing in the day the Lord has made.

To be clear, I'm not like that. I need 200 cc of strong fair-trade coffee and a personal invitation from the Holy Spirit before I drag my body back to the land of the living. Mama likes her sleep. It's important to keep that in mind throughout this chapter because I am about to introduce you to a practice I refer to as my "Reclaim the Morning" liturgy. In fact, there is a part of me that feels a bit shamefaced, erecting part of my life's work on a foundational practice so far outside of how I'm wired. But perhaps that's how you can trust it works. This single daily habit has shifted my life, and I hope it keeps you afloat until you can find your own redemptive liturgy to lean into your day on purpose.

Speaking of purpose, you might have to walk a bit of a mental tightrope as I share how to reclaim the morning. We're dancing along the edge of life hack territory, where the ultimate goal is productivity, optimization, and success. The temptation will be to drift back into that space of external formation where you focus on me as another voice telling you how to live. Tread carefully because I'm no Gwyneth Paltrow, and this isn't a goop moment. You don't have to conform to my way of living. This is a suggestion, albeit a strong one. If you try the practice on and it feels like wearing someone else's bra, take it off. Also, ew. All I ask is that you give it a fair shot because I've seen the power of this liturgy in my clients' lives, and I don't want you to miss it. This is important.

In its most basic form, Reclaim the Morning is a daily journaling practice to help you stay centered and combat dissociation. It works for absolutely anyone and can be done in less than thirty minutes if that's all the time you have. I'm going to flesh out some additional details about the how and when of it all to help you maximize the experience. But try not to overcomplicate what we're doing. Part of the power is in its simplicity. It doesn't take much to begin, so you can get started as soon as possible—like tomorrow morning. Put it on your calendar.

But before I get into the specifics, let me take you back to where it all started. Because if you're going to be invited into a new practice, especially one that involves potential early wake-ups or delayed caffeine intake (spoiler alert), you deserve to know the why behind it. Reclaim the Morning first started in the place where most great things begin: New York City.

HOW IT ALL STARTED

If you've never had the dual pleasure and pain of being a New Yorker, let me give you a little context. New York City is loud. I don't mean in that charming way that feels like a Nora Ephron movie. In real life, Meg Ryan doesn't skip into a corner bookshop to the gentle hum and drumbeat of busy Manhattan street sounds. Most days New York is a Scorsese film. Think *Gangs of New York* or *The Wolf of Wall Street*. There is the constant bang and clang of construction sites, investment bankers yelling unintelligibly into cell phones, and the perpetual screech of Ubers and Lyfts shuttling disheveled New Yorkers around the city. It's sonic mayhem.

And to be fair, it's glorious. Transplants to New York come for the bagels and stay for the noise. It's a phenomenal place to live. But it's also hard to focus and hear yourself think. And as a New Yorker, you find yourself trying to drown out not just the literal noise of urban life, but also the figurative din that accompanies living at the nexus of social innovation. There is a nearly audible *thump thump thump* from the constant production of cultural goods. Around every corner, someone is rushing somewhere to make something of the world in tech, the arts, business, and more. It's fast-paced, high-pressure, and *loud*.

Which is why in the city, if you want to be a person of distinction, you have to hunt for silence and solitude with the persistence of Wile E. Coyote chasing after the Road Runner. Otherwise, you'll be formed into the same kind of person everyone around you is becoming. The current will sweep you up and take you downstream with all the rest of the salmon.

It's in this reality of New York that Reclaim the Morning was born. My then-pastor, Jon Tyson, was trying to help our congregation of young, influential New Yorkers live upstream.* He wanted to invite us into a daily habit that would help us manage our energy and put God as the primary voice informing how we lived our day. In the city that never sleeps, New Yorkers often stay up late, running on fumes to accomplish all they can. Time with God could easily get wedged into late-night Bible studies or sleepy prayers after wild evenings partying with other hipsters. He called on us to "reclaim the morning." That meant giving God our firstfruits—waking up early to pray, read Scripture, or sit in silence before launching into the day.

I was obsessed. Right away, reclaiming the morning felt powerful. It was like a throwback to youth ministry days when having

---

* Fun fact: Jon Tyson is the pastor of Church of the City New York. I had the privilege of working with him as a communications director and ministry strategist for Trinity Grace Church, a network of parish churches he planted in the early 2000s. Jon also officiated the marriage for me and my hubby.

a "quiet time" was all the rage.[†] If you're not familiar, there was a generational wave of Christianity where teenagers routinely woke up around six in the morning, grabbed their *True Love Waits* Bibles, and read Scripture for at least thirty minutes before hopping on the bus to school. I think this was around the same time that Christian boy bands were a thing and WWJD (What would Jesus do?) bracelets were making the rounds. Anyway, at some point, we all stopped promoting the idea of having a quiet time. Morning devotionals became uncool as the pendulum swung from authentic time with God toward legalism and behavior management.

But as a twentysomething living in New York, adopting the practice felt subversive and rejuvenating. Reclaiming the morning was like rediscovering an old habit from another time when my soul felt open and ready to be formed. And it wasn't just the practice but the phrase itself. It invoked a sense of taking back control. It gave off big Maxine Waters energy, like I was sitting before the House of Representatives stating, "I'm reclaiming my time." I was desperate to sit in the driver's seat of my life, and it felt proactive.

It also felt magical to start my day slowly, easing into the world rather than rushing into the day. The volume of New York is rivaled only by its speed. Any New Yorker will tell you that in the city, if you don't run, you get run over—quickly. You learn to live at eighty miles an hour—the kind of hurry John Mark Comer calls "a form of violence on the soul."[1] But reclaiming the morning meant a daily chance to slow down, reset, and inch into life with perspective and grace.

---

† Remember when that was a thing? Or am I telling my age and denomination again? Let's bring back the devotional!

WHY RECLAIM THE MORNING *NOW*?

As I started to grow in the practice, I noticed the primary benefit for me was not solely spiritual growth, which is why I'm sharing it with you now. Many of my clients who are not Christian have adopted this practice despite the obvious overlap here in terms of spiritual development. If you are a woman of faith, you'll probably find that reclaiming the morning does help you reconnect to God. Something about the quiet and honest confrontation of the self helps draw us closer to God. He meets us in the quiet place. He is the author of our lives, so it should be no surprise that in silence and solitude, we find he is the voice calling us into our purpose.

But for our purposes, let's consider spiritual growth to be a happy accident. After all, I'm not your pastor or a theologian. I only minored in biblical studies during college. My primary training and orientation here is psychological, so I'll stay in my lane as your two-hundred-page quasi–life coach. Therefore, I'm encouraging you to reclaim the morning because of how it impacts your ability to live intentionally. It's a daily opportunity to decide who you are becoming, rather than to flail around in the water hoping things get better. It's a chance to listen to who you want to be.

In *Let Your Life Speak*, Parker J. Palmer wrote, "Before I can tell my life what I want to do with it, I must listen to my life telling me who I am. I must listen for the truths and values at the heart of my own identity, not the standards by which I *must* live—but the standards by which I cannot help but live if I am living my own life."[2] Reclaiming the morning is your chance to listen to your life speak. That's why I am so committed to this practice now both for myself and my clients.

We spent a great deal of time talking about liturgies in the last chapters, and I've found that how you start your day can determine the full trajectory of where it ends. This redemptive liturgy I'm encouraging you to adopt can reset the bounds of how your day evolves. Remember those limiting beliefs we talked about in chapter 1 that keep us focused on a life of significance? By reclaiming the morning, we intentionally push back against the limiting narratives that we are the culmination of where we work, who we love, or what we possess. We need to consciously insert a new narrative, or we'll believe the lies. When you reclaim the morning, you get to define yourself—for yourself—each and every day.

It's also a powerful way to build up courage so that when you go out into the world, you can be strong enough to swim against the demands of the culture. In this structured, sacred space, you can safely form your identity without worrying what other people think or have to say about it. And the confidence that comes from that practice builds your self-esteem muscle so you can begin to assert who you are in the world and enthusiastically construct your version of the good life.

Let's get into the details of how to get started.

BASIC PREPARATION

Reclaiming the morning actually starts the night before as you prepare to make the most of your time alone the next day. Calculate how much sleep you need on an average night, and then set a bedtime for yourself that sounds reasonable. Here's the kicker: Actually go to bed on time. I don't know about you, but it's about as hard to put me to bed as a teething toddler. I get a burst of energy around nine o' clock and want to use that time to do "all the things." I'm the type of person who thinks, *Ten o' clock would be a great time to reorganize my family photo albums!* But I've learned to create a wind-down routine in the evening that encourages me to go to sleep. If I'm faithful to my nighttime routine, waking up isn't as challenging.

If you're in search of ideas for how to create a simple evening routine for yourself that will ease you into sleep, here is my process to help jump-start your thinking:

8:15 P.M. Bedtime routine with my son (bath, books, and prayer)

8:45 P.M. Tidy up the house and reset for the morning (locate everything I'll need to have a strong start)

9:00 P.M. Shower and wash my face (make it indulgent with a luxe skincare set if I can financially splurge that month)

9:20 P.M. Brush and floss my teeth‡ (this feels like punishment, by the way)

9:30 P.M. Put my phone in the drawer and read one of the thirty-five books on my nightstand

9:45 P.M. Lights out

What kind of wind-down routine would work for you? Consider which activities help you slow down in the evening and more quickly fall asleep.

---

‡ Why is flossing so hard to do consistently? The late comedian Mitch Hedberg had a joke saying he knew how hard it was to quit smoking. It's just as hard as it is to start flossing. Truer words have never been said.

If you're someone who ruminates and is "in your head" a lot, the evening is a great time to inject a liturgy into your life that helps you get in touch with your body. I find that doing anything slow and tactile helps the body prepare to sleep. I like a hot shower and/or a slow ten minutes spent washing my face with strongly scented products to cue my brain that it's time to rest. Also, reducing screen time close to bedtime is critical. Most sleep experts caution against the use of screens if you're struggling to fall asleep, because the blue light emitted from electronic devices can suppress natural melatonin levels. Melatonin is the hormone in your body that helps control your sleep and wake cycles. Beyond falling asleep, screens can also mess with the *quality* of your sleep, affecting slow-wave and REM (rapid eye movement) cycles that lead your body to feel refreshed.

Take a moment to formulate a plan for tonight. Then keep reading for the specifics of what you'll do when you wake.

HOW TO RECLAIM THE MORNING

First, start by getting up thirty minutes before your usual wake-up time so you can carve out space to be alone. If you typically wake up early but tend to spend the time putzing around in an undirected way, keep your same rise-and-shine time. Don't bother waking up earlier; just wake up with a mission. The numbers on the clock aren't sacred, so please don't get caught up in thinking one time is more opportune than another. You don't have to be part of the five a.m. club if that's not your jam. All you need is to wake up early enough to have a half hour of dedicated time alone without anyone bothering you. You also want to avoid your Reclaim the Morning time running into your daily prep activities, like showering or deciding what you'll wear for the day. If you can't imagine a full half hour at this point, I hear you. Start smaller. Allison Fallon, author of *The Power of Writing It Down*, wrote, "Research shows that writing for as little as twenty minutes a day for four days in a row can measurably improve your mood."[3] So start with twenty minutes . . . or fifteen . . . or even ten. Just get started.

I highly recommend (read: insist) you avoid checking your phone for messages, emails, or social media when you first wake. A quick glance at your phone is one of the fastest ways to hijack your attention and send those neurons blazing down familiar neural pathways where you're focused on external concerns. The goal of this sacred morning time is for you to encounter and confront your authentic self without anyone else's influence, so keep those voices at bay as long as possible. This might mean you need to get an old-school alarm clock to wake you so Alexa is not the one beckoning you immediately upon waking.

Once you get out of bed, head to a private space where you can write two to three pages of stream of conscious thought. Write about anything and everything that comes to mind. If you don't know what to write, start scribbling, "I don't know what to write. I don't know what to write. I don't know . . ." until something emerges for you. There is no wrong way to do it. You're allowed to write down whatever comes to mind and follow your thoughts to wherever they might wander. For our purposes, the journey is the destination. I know that sounds very Yoda-like, but it's the truest way I can say it. The whole point is to be and explore what matters to you. Sometimes you'll have to wade through piles of thoughts and beliefs you've adopted from other people before you can unearth what you really think about your life. That's okay. Take your time.

My mind bounces all over the place during these morning sessions. Sometimes I'm stuck in an emotion or preoccupied with a specific issue in my life I'm trying to resolve, so I'll write about that. Other times I have a big decision coming up, so I'll process the pros and cons. Sometimes I write stories, business ideas, or poems. Most days I come to the page without an agenda, allowing my mind to unravel itself. I'll write about the things that are bringing me joy or capturing my hopes and anxieties of the season.

Over time, as you write, notice what lands on the page. Do you find yourself regularly writing about old wounds that have not healed? Are you focused on certain recurring anxieties that need to be addressed? Do you have latent desires that remain unexplored? Get curious about the woman you are. Don't judge what's on the page. Just notice it. As you observe yourself in print day after day, you'll begin to see more clearly the picture of who this woman is outside of the influence of others. My clients usually start with a blurred outline of who they are, and over time the lines become clearer as they start to sketch in more details. Be gracious toward the woman you see on the page, and pay attention to what needs she's expressing so you can help her be more fully realized.

I'm going to leave it at that because the more I explain, the further I push you from the purpose of this time. The practice's power is in the lack of structure and the simplicity of intention. Just be and use the page to capture what you find. If it feels open and a bit unwieldy, you've nailed it. After all, we're essentially talking about contemplative practice. My attempts to put any structure around it are somewhat futile. As Thomas Merton wrote in *New Seeds of Contemplation*, "Contemplation cannot be taught. It cannot even be clearly explained. It can only be hinted at, suggested, pointed to, symbolized. The more objectively and scientifically one tries to analyze it, the more he empties it of its real content, for this experience is beyond the reach of verbalization and of rationalization."[4] Given this, my best guidance is only to suggest you try it and see what happens.

By the way, my Reclaim the Morning practice is one of the reasons you're reading this book. In the first half of 2020, I noticed my journal pages were filled with desires to put my life-planning process to the page so I could help more women figure out their life purpose. It showed up day after day, and I finally had to confront that I was not honoring a desire to write a book. The noise of my daily life usually drowned out the whisper of this childhood hope to become an author, but it was screaming from every page I wrote in the morning. The liturgy of journaling helped me hold my deep internal desire in higher regard so I could start to put action behind the life I was waiting to live.

What might your little voice be screaming to do? Find it on the page.

Pro-Tips

The most important part of reclaiming the morning is to get started quickly, so don't overthink it. But if you want to make the time even more valuable, here are some ideas for how you can upgrade the experience and optimize your time:

1. **MAKE THE EXPERIENCE LUXURIOUS.** Snuggle up in your favorite blanket, light a scented candle, or write your morning thoughts in a leather journal with a special pen.

Do whatever helps you feel like this time is an indulgence. That act of self-care will keep you running back to this sacred moment day after day and retrain your brain to believe that you are worthy of this alone time. Waking up early doesn't have to feel like a punishment or "one more thing" to do so you can be productive. Reframe your morning time as a special treat you give yourself every day.

2. **AVOID STIMULANTS BEFORE YOU WRITE.** That means hold off on the coffee and sugar until you have a couple of pages written. I'm obsessed with coffee, so I hate to be a killjoy. Making my morning cup is one of the best parts of my day. However, I've found that caffeine and sugar stimulate my mind too much, making it harder to focus and maintain the reflective, meditative state that makes reclaiming the morning so valuable. Test this out for yourself to see what impact your morning coffee has on you. Do you feel scattered mentally, unable to focus after drinking a mug of coffee? If so, try holding off and replacing your morning brew with something else. I like the comfort of a warm cup, so I drink hot water with a little lemon juice or a decaffeinated tea while I'm writing. Then I make a cup of coffee as my treat after breakfast to signal that it's time to dive into the day.

3. **EMPTY BEFORE YOU FILL.** Integrating a physical, spiritual, or educational practice is a great addition to the Reclaim the Morning liturgy if you want to extend the time. Some of my clients pair their journaling with stretching, a meditation app, reading scripture, or enjoying a book. Just remember to write first so you can dump what's on your mind before you take in anything new.

The goal is to hear your own voice first and then receive what the world has for you in a position of being more grounded and in touch with who you are.

REASONS YOU'LL NEVER DO THIS

Okay, so let's be honest with one another. Reclaiming the morning sounds like a great idea. You're totally on board. Or maybe you're side-eyeing me because I said you can't drink coffee before you start, and now you don't want to hear anything more from me. If that's the deal breaker for you, by the way, do whatever you want. I'm not your mom. Drink coffee if you want to drink coffee. I'm only sharing what I've learned, so you have to decide how it will affect you. But even if you have full intention to start this practice, here's what will get in your way.

You're going to say:

- **"I'M NOT A MORNING PERSON."** Well neither am I, remember? This isn't about waking up before the sun rises or the early bird getting the worm. This is about reorienting your life to hop out of the rhythm of significance-seeking every single day so you can intentionally pay attention to what you want. If that has to happen at ten thirty because you can't open your eyes before that, fine. Just reclaim the morning before you do anything else.
- **"I HAVE KIDS. ARE YOU CRAZY?"** I'm crazy like a fox. Reclaim the Morning is a great opportunity to teach your children that you value yourself and that quiet is important. As you retrain your own mind, train them too. If

they tend to distract you, either send them back to their rooms or set them up near you with their own Reclaim the Morning station. Grab crayons and markers for them to draw or hand them some Play-doh. Tell them you're playing a game to see how long they can be quiet. Make it fun with a snack. Kids love that kind of stuff. If they absolutely can't be quiet, try to do this before they wake by getting yourself a small reading lamp and reclaiming the morning from your bed like a stealth self-care ninja.

- **"I'M MORE PRODUCTIVE AT NIGHT. CAN I DO IT THEN?"** No. This isn't about productivity. This is about framing your day, and that starts with the morning. If you want to add in some elaborate evening rhythm, that's fine with me. Do you, boo. But make sure you keep your Reclaim the Morning time.

- **"THIS SOUNDS LIKE SOMETHING ONLY MEN HAVE THE LUXURY OF DOING."** I hear you on this one. For the past year, I've been in an online community of more than fifteen hundred female entrepreneurs, and I regularly hear them gripe about male patriarchy and the privilege to spend two hours every morning on themselves. I really do hear you. And I've also found this to be an excuse. First, I'm not asking you to spend two hours. You can spend fifteen minutes, and this will still be effective. More time is only better, but it's not required. Second, I think it's easy to make excuses for ourselves. Yes, you will have trade-offs. You can't do certain things, and it will require more prep in the evening on other activities. But this is important for you. Make the time.

- **"I DON'T LIVE ALONE. WHERE CAN I DO THIS?"** You don't need a lot of space. Use a closet if that's all you have.

Or use a natural light lamp to wake and then stay in bed to journal so you don't disrupt Sleeping Beauty next to you. This is also a great time to practice asserting your needs. Share with your roommate or partner why this time is valuable to you and what impact it might have on your life if you can make it happen. Let them support you rather than be an obstacle to the time.

RESULTS MAY VARY

I can't wait to see how your energy for the day and sense of self begin to shift as you start this practice. You don't have to get it all perfect right off the bat. Like dissociation, the power in the liturgy is in the cumulative effect. Try it out for a few weeks and see if anything emerges. It takes twenty-one days to build a habit. The results might surprise you.

You might find that you are like my client Lydia. She shared that starting this practice didn't just change her morning; it changed her whole day. Before we met, she already had a journaling practice, but most days it felt compulsory. Waking up for "self-care" felt like something she "should do" to help manage anxiety or be more productive. Previously she'd used a template, following a prescriptive pattern like writing a daily gratitude list in order to model the habits of "highly successful people." Even though it was helpful, it felt like a to-do. She was "doing" self-care. When she started to reclaim the morning, she felt free. The stream of consciousness writing helped her focus on being, not doing, and it quickly became an activity she looked forward to each day. I hope you have a similar result.

Friend, you are ready. We've laid the foundation. In the next section we'll begin to cobble together your life purpose so you can lift your head out of the water. We'll start by defining what a solid life purpose looks like, and then we'll put language to what you do exceedingly well. By the end of this book, I'm hoping you can begin to value the incredible woman God created you to be.

I can't wait for you to meet her.

LIFE ASSESSMENT

Before you head into the next section, take some time to reflect on where you are now. We're going to cover a lot of ground, so let's take stock of how your life is going. Grab a notebook and use your new Reclaim the Morning time to practice personalizing what you're reading.

Spend time answering the following four clarifying questions, taking into account all of your life buckets (self, relationships, career, spirituality, and global engagement).

(1) **HOW AM I CURRENTLY THRIVING?** These are areas to protect and optimize.

(2) **HOW AM I CURRENTLY STRIVING?** These are areas to change or clarify.

(3) **WHAT IS MY DISSATISFACTION COSTING ME?** Note the time, energy, or financial costs associated with striving.

(4) **AM I READY TO CHANGE?** Yes or no.

Download this worksheet and other tools to help you start living now at chaneldokun.com/lifestartsnow

part two

GETTING
YOUR HEAD
ABOVE WATER

six

REDEFINING YOUR PURPOSE

Once you know who you are, it's
easier to refute who you aren't.

LUVVIE AJAYI JONES, *PROFESSIONAL TROUBLEMAKER*

All right, let's get your head above water.

We keep talking about letting go of living someone else's version of the good life, but do you have an idea of your own? Remember what James K. A. Smith said: Our lives bend toward the image of flourishing that has most captured our imaginations. If our aim is to move you away from significance-seeking, and closer to your authentic life of consequence, we need a compelling vision that is rich with details to arrest your heart. Only then can you begin to move away from the person others may want you to be and closer to who you are.

And this is the tricky part of what we're going to do next. This part of the book may feel a bit like drinking from a fire hose, because I want to inundate you with details to help you flesh out your unique vision of thriving. We're trying to woo your heart. And to be honest, you're a saucy little minx who is not easily swayed. If we want you to long for something different than the life you've been pursuing, we need the alternative vision to be detailed, attractive, and robust.

So stick with me. At times what I'm asking you to consider will feel disjointed. That's okay. Trust the process. Every piece of what I'm inviting you to explore will help add perspective and color so you can begin envisioning *your* life. At first this might feel underwhelming because the information you're gathering is so familiar. The little parts of who you are don't seem to amount to much. And part of you will want to run back to the other versions of flourishing that first led you to slowly drown in the shallow water. Don't turn tail and run.

With time we'll transform the ordinary into the extraordinary. As you accumulate more and more data about who you are, you'll begin to see the powerful life you have waiting just under your nose. And what is that powerful life? What does it mean to thrive? I would argue that flourishing, for you, looks like living according to your original design. Thriving is operating the way you were intended.

REDEFINING THE GOOD LIFE

Isn't that true of most things? We call something *good* or *perfect* when it does what it was meant to do. For example, my iPhone is a powerful device that can do a lot of things. It makes an excellent paperweight, a potential hammer, and even a pretty stellar camera for me, an amateur photographer. But if my iPhone doesn't make or receive calls—if it doesn't send text messages or load any apps—I would say it's a pretty crummy phone. If it's failing to do what it was created for, it's useful but not good. I don't need an average paperweight. I need an extraordinary phone. Likewise, you will be living the good life when you're living *your* good life. Thriving looks like becoming who you were always meant to be.

This is a delicate point—and maybe the idea of becoming who you are doesn't jibe with you at all. Maybe somewhere along the line you internalized the lie that you are fundamentally broken, flawed, or ordinary. And you want to get as far away from the life you fear you're meant to live as possible. But I have to argue that I think your starting assumption is wrong. At baseline, I know you are phenomenal.

Let me show my cards a bit and reveal two presuppositions I bring to all of my work with clients. These two beliefs shape how I engage the search for purpose, so I want to be explicit with you. Fair warning that you may not agree with me, and that's okay. If you've been disillusioned by people of faith or if you've decided spirituality is not a significant part of your life, my approach and process will work for you too. But I want to be transparent about where I'm coming from in case this unblocks some of the difficulty you've had with finding your purpose up to this point. Take what is helpful and leave the rest as you decide how you envision your purpose.*

---

* This is actually a powerful sign of your emotional maturity. In therapy we say that the ability to hold on to oneself in the face of conflicting ideals—to be "well-differentiated"—is a sign of personal growth. So bravo if you can disagree and not lose yourself in the gap of opinions.

First, I believe you aren't an accident; you were *created*. Regardless of the circumstances under which you were conceived, you were intentionally made, knit together in your mother's womb, and handcrafted by God. And if you agree that's true, it will require an important reorientation in your search for meaning. Because if God created you, then he is the one who determines what the good life looks like for you. The Creator sets the vision for the creation. Eventually you'll have to submit to God's version of what thriving looks like for you. We all do. Many of us would like to believe Jesus is less like the author of our lives and more like the ultimate life coach, running alongside us and giving a periodic ego boost as we try to live the life we want. But like Paul David Tripp wrote in *New Morning Mercies*, "He has never promised us that he will deliver to us our personal definition of the good life."[1] That's not how any of this works.

I know that may sound like a downer. And I would be worried about what that means for my fulfillment, too, if I didn't have this second presupposition about the world: I know God's purpose for you is good. In fact, I think it's best. I think he knows you better than you know yourself because he made you, and I think his heart is to love you and show you kindness. Isaiah 30:18 tells us that God "longs to be gracious to you" and "show you compassion." Because God is good, I trust, and I hope you'll trust, too, that when you submit your plans to what God has in mind for you, you'll find the most fulfilling pathway to your purpose. Flourishing is fulfilling your original design.

This is another reason why we need courage to be nobody—because for a moment I'm going to need you to go out on a limb. You're going to have to trust that if you surrender what you've come to believe is the best life for yourself, and then you settle into the life you were designed to live, everything will be okay. That's been true for my clients, and it's certainly been true for me. Before I discovered my purpose, I crafted whole lives for myself that I thought would be best, shaped by external ideas for success. I thought there were men I should have married, careers I was meant to pursue, and experiences I was destined to have. But I found my best version of the good life when I let go of the ones that truly never fit.

So what does a thriving life look like for you? Do you know why you exist?

The Japanese call it your *ikigai*, and the French say it's your *raison d'être*. Both essentially mean your "reason for being." You might have thought of this as your life's calling or your vocation. Or you might never have thought of it at all. It's easy to walk through life focused on specific goals here and there, without ever considering a deeper meaning behind the narrative your life is telling.

But you need to examine your existence and tap into your core reason for being. We all have a purpose, but whether or not we've identified it is the real question. Here's another way to think of it: Do you have a primary calling that drives your life and determines how you experience the world around you? Often we have an underlying purpose that is driving our actions without our knowing it. Getting to the place where we can not only amplify our awareness of our purpose but also begin to live more intentionally into it is the key.

So let me ask another way, assuming you've given some modicum of thought to why you're on the planet. Have you ever put language to your calling? Have you reached into the vast container of all possible meaning, grabbed a handful of purpose for yourself, and wrapped words around what makes you, *you*? If not, now is the time. Because if you want to stop living someone else's version of the good life and step into your own, you need a clear articulation of what thriving looks like for you.

Remember? I gave away the secret to what makes a meaningful life back in chapter 1. I told you that to stop drowning in shallow water, you need to lift up your head and stand in the fullness of your unique identity. As you uncover the what and the why of your life, you'll stop getting caught in the trap of pursuing someone else's version of significance.

But don't panic. We're in this together. We're going to get clarity on your life purpose throughout this next section so you can have a North Star guiding you toward the life you're meant to live. I'll supply you with language to communicate your why so you can assert who you are to others and continually make choices in line with that identity.

So let's get started.

AN EXPANSION OF PURPOSE

When a woman comes to me asking for clarity on her calling, I find she has usually reduced a three-part question into one question or conundrum. Maybe you've done the same. She may ask, "What is my life purpose?" or "Why do I exist?" But here are the three things I hear her trying to unpack behind one monster existential question:

1. **"WHO AM I?"** She wants to uncover more of her identity so she can express who she is in the world. She wants to know how to distinguish herself in a relationship,

community, or organization so she can make a mark on society. She also wants to feel known not only by others but also by herself, growing in confidence and self-compassion. One woman I worked with put it like this. She said, "Chanel, I want to connect the dots. I want to develop a more integrated personal and professional identity instead of feeling like my life is a bunch of random pieces. And I want to know (and like) the real me."

2. **"WHERE AM I HEADED?"** Part of understanding her life purpose is answering this question about direction. She wants to know where her life is going so she can consistently pursue a target. Clients often point to a need for a "North Star" or guiding mission to give intention to their lives.

3. **"HOW DO I GET THERE?"** Lastly, she wants a plan. Big vision is great, but she wants to outline the specific action steps she can take to move toward her life objective. One client wrote, "I want to know not just *what* I want out of life but *how* to get it."

These are all great questions. More than that, they are all necessary components that make up what it means to have clarity on one's life purpose: identity, direction, and action.

You can't isolate any one part from the other. Let's say you start executing a plan or taking action on a goal that is disconnected from your identity and life direction. You'll end up in a situation that might be successful, but it also might be unsustainable or unfulfilling. Or if you focus only on direction, without a plan of action or a strong sense of who you are, you can end up stalled, dreaming of a life you'll never live. Finally, if you prioritize only identity development, without vision or action, you'll spend all your time navel-gazing but never applying any of who you are to the world around you. It's a both/and situation. We'll need to get to the bottom of each of these questions in order for you to have a robust sense of who you are and what you're meant to do in the world.

THE DIFFERENCE BETWEEN LIFE COACHING AND LIFE PLANNING

I have to slow you down here because, unfortunately, most women start with the last question. They immediately want to hop to an action plan to reach their big goals. Not us. We're going to begin at the beginning, and when we get to the end, we'll stop. It seems obvious, but I can't tell you how many women I work with who have wasted years of time and money because they started in the wrong place. Fed up with their present circumstances, they just start executing on a new life goal.

For example, they hate their job, so they apply for a bunch of new opportunities or try launching their own business. They're exhausted by life in New York City, so they start making plans to move across the country to Los Angeles. They are sick of being single, so they sign up for all the dating websites they can find. This is usually when they hire a life coach. *Help me become the version of myself I want to be!*

Have you ever done this? Have you hired a coach or bought a book to help you develop a plan or program to become something else? I know I have. Maybe that's why you're reading this book now.

But can I ask you something? How would a woman know if these goals—the new business, the move, or chasing a relationship—are the right goals for her to pursue? How would *you* know if those were *your* goals? Let's think about it. What if you got halfway down the path of starting that new business and then realized you're not wired to be an entrepreneur? Or what if you moved to another city, but it turned out your boyfriend was the one making you miserable, not your apartment? What if the real reason you haven't been able to get a date is because you've never dealt with your past trauma and you keep sabotaging every potential prospect to protect yourself from getting hurt again? Before taking action, you need perspective. Perspective provides the necessary parameters for developing a goal.

That's the primary difference between life coaching and life planning. While life coaching puts a greater emphasis on achieving linear goals, life planning honors the foundational questions that inform your life objectives. We get perspective first on who you are and where you want to go before catalyzing you to take action. The benefit is that you have more certainty (and thereby more courage to take risks) because you know that your plans are rooted in the truth of who you are and what you want. It's living out of the consequence of your identity rather than taking action to make you feel significant. It's the definition of inside-out living.

A NEW DEFINITION OF PURPOSE

So let's get back to your life purpose. As you gain clarity on why you exist in the world, we're going to focus on the three afore-mentioned pieces of identity, direction, and action. To do that, I want you to first reframe how you think of your *ikigai*.

Often when people talk about purpose, they refer to it as a

mission to accomplish. It's a big mark they are hoping to make "out there" on the world or an overarching goal they want to check off their list. This way of thinking can create a "nailed it or failed it" dynamic in their lives. Anything short of completing their life purpose feels like failure or an undone task. *I'm supposed to do something with my life, and I haven't yet. Woe is me.* This generates a perpetual sense of urgency to cross *purpose* off the list. Can you feel the significance vibes all over that way of thinking? In that kind of framework, your life purpose is something you *do*.

That way of life isn't for us. We are women of consequence—which means we show up in the world as our full selves, and as a *consequence* of our being, there are results. Your greatest impact comes from your *being*, not your *doing*. Every day that you show up as an immovable force in your authentic self, the world has to organize itself around you. Like a stone in a riverbed, the world flows and adjusts to how you take shape, and that is how you make a splash. Do you feel the difference?

This is why your ordinary life matters. You may have counted yourself out already. Maybe you think you're not all that special. You're drowning and you haven't achieved much. But whether you own it or not, the entire river of culture is moving around you. What shape are you giving it? How are you impacting the flow of this generation?

It's hard to know. And that's why when I talk about finding your unique purpose, instead of giving a definition, I describe your purpose as a place. It's as though you can locate your *raison d'être* on a map. I say your life purpose lies at the intersection of your talents, your heart, and your influence. Those are the co-ordinates. And once you have them, you can find your way back to your true self again and again.

We'll dive into your talents, heart, and influence in greater detail later, but notice how each of these coordinates on our life map refers to the core clarity questions related to identity, direction, and action I mentioned at the start of this chapter. Knowing your talents is a targeted way of saying we have distilled who you are in the world into clear language that uniquely describes you. Honoring and activating your heart provides us with direction so we have a compelling vision for your life that arouses your passions. Learning how to steward your influence breaks you out of the inertia of daily living to take continual action toward engaging the world around you in a purposeful way. Each piece moves us closer toward our central goal of helping you stop drowning by standing in your unique purpose.

Once you've located your purpose, you'll be able to write a clear life purpose statement you can use to keep you on the path God has marked out for you. Like plugging an address into a GPS, writing down your life purpose statement can help populate the turn-by-turn directions to guide you toward your ultimate life vision. The next chapters will help you uncover your talents (identity), heart (direction), and influence (action) so that your unique life purpose becomes clear and you can get it down on paper and start deciding how you're going to live in alignment with where you're headed.

THE ANATOMY OF A GOOD LIFE PURPOSE STATEMENT

But hold up. Pop quiz, hotshot: Why do you exist . . . now?

Let's write down your current operating life purpose statement so we have something to compare it to later after you've worked through my framework. It doesn't have to be perfect. If it was spot-on, you wouldn't be bothering to read this book because you'd be out there living your best life. We're at the beginning of the process, so if it's not inspiring to you yet, that's okay. Just try to articulate in one sentence why you exist. Take less than two minutes to write down what Anne Lamott would call a crummy first draft.[†] As we go through the next chapters, I'm going to help you learn more about yourself so you can expand on this statement and refine it to accuracy. But right now, what are we working with?

Why I exist: _____

_____[‡]

If you're like many of the women I've worked with, you probably wrote down something like:

- I exist to help people feel known and appreciated.
- I exist to be a light.
- I exist to encourage others and remind them of who God is.
- I exist to make this world a better place.
- I exist to be a support to my friends and family.

I've got to be honest. These statements aren't terrible. They're from real women I've worked with before they started the

---

[†] For the record, Anne Lamott does not call our first drafts crummy. She uses a more colorful word that I scream out every time Beyoncé releases a new line of Ivy Park clothing with Adidas that sells out in less than forty-five seconds (and before I can place my order). Read Lamott's *Bird by Bird* if you want to know exactly what she says.

[‡] Want bonus points? I'd love to read your current life purpose statement. Send it to me and get resources through the book hub at chaneldokun.com/lifestartsnow.

life-planning process. In fact, some are pretty good. But I want to upgrade you a little bit, the way Beyoncé did for Jay-Z. I mean, you're good now, but let's make you great.

When I help my clients discover their life purpose, here's what I look for in a statement to know whether or not we've nailed it. First, I want to make sure the statement is large enough to encompass all areas of their life. Remember how we talked about the temptation to view our vocation and purpose solely through the lens of career or through our relationships? If the statement can be applied to all five of our life buckets (self, relationships, career, spirituality, and global engagement), I know we have a statement that honors the fullness of who the woman is.

Next, a strong life purpose statement is also specific, meaning it's not so vague that it could apply to absolutely anyone. A common answer women give to the question "Why do you exist?" is to say something along the lines of "I exist to love others" or "I exist to be a good person." My favorite response is, "I'm here to serve God." Or sometimes people will be a little more artful and say something like, "My purpose is to be a light, burning with a passion to serve others."

Look, I'm not here to rain on your poetic purpose parade, but those kinds of statements don't cut it. I usually respond gently with "Well, congratulations, you're a human!" Okay, maybe that's not so gentle.[§] But you get my point. I want to rattle them a bit so they can acknowledge how lost they still are with these kinds of sentimental statements—because there is nothing unique about existing to serve God or love people or be kind. As Kristen Bell's character, Eleanor, said on *The Good Place*, "Ya basic!"[2]

---

§ I'm nothing if not subtle.

Everyone is here for those things. Let's file them under "true but not helpful."

So you're here to love others. *How* do you do that? Your life purpose needs to be specific enough that it can serve as a guide to move you out into the world. If you're over here living in Vague City, pay extra attention in the next chapter about illuminating your talents so you can pick up some clues and narrow your purpose a little more. I've got you.

Lastly, a life purpose statement needs to be flexible, meaning it can evolve throughout the course of time. One of my favorite parts of life planning is that when we develop a plan for a client, it doesn't just apply to one particular season, relationship status, career journey, or location. We want a statement that can shape-shift and apply to the many changes that the average life endures. For example, my life purpose statement applied when I was single and living in New York City. It still applies now as a married mom in Atlanta, shuttling my kid to soccer practice and doctors' appointments. Your statement needs to ride with you.

Now let me show you the *after* versions. (I've already told you about my love of Joanna Gaines, so imagine I'm standing next to her husband, Chip, down in Waco and we're about to give you the big reveal.) Here are some of the life purpose statements my clients have discovered through their coaching sessions with me:

- I exist to express transcendent joy and create moments that cultivate wonder and capture beauty.
- I exist to bring actionable discernment and encouragement to others in order to move toward mental, physical, or spiritual growth.

- I exist to honor and care for my community by creating opportunities to foster happiness and achievement.
- I exist to identify brokenness and share ideas to empower wholeness and facilitate cultural transformation.

That last one is mine, by the way. I know it sounds lofty, but it's true, and it's something I do in every part of my life, every single day. Do you hear the difference? Embedded in each of these statements from my clients is rich potential for application. You can also hear ever so slightly how each woman is different. Even if they had some commonality of talents, they probably wouldn't apply them the same way because their ambitions are unique. I want to create that level of distinction for you.

Let me throw in one more pro tip on life purpose statements. I wasn't originally going to get into this, but I feel like since you've made it through chapter 4's philosophy lesson and still remember what *teleological* means, you can handle this. (Reminder: *Teleological* means purposeful or intentional, in case your eyes were glazed over at that part of the book.) I want to talk about a key indicator of your life purpose that you might not think is important.

Here it goes: Your life purpose can't be about you.

LEARNING TO LIVE BEYOND YOURSELF

Hear me out on this. I know we're talking about how to help you live out *your* version of the good life. And we're talking about getting you more fulfillment and satisfaction so you can stop drowning. But the interesting truth is that you won't be fulfilled until you find something bigger than yourself to live for. Don't just take my word for it. Blame psychologist Abraham Maslow.

Back in 1943, Maslow published a paper called "A Theory of Human Motivation." He was trying to describe human behavior and what motivates people to act. In psychology we often refer to his work as the human hierarchy of needs. You've probably seen a pyramid representing his theory at some point in your life.

At the bottom of the pyramid, he started out with basic stuff that you need for survival—like food, water, and shelter. Your first urge in life is to address these physiological needs. Once you have stuff like sleep down pat, you can move up the pyramid— now focusing on needs like safety, belonging to community, and then self-esteem. Near the top of the pyramid is self-actualization, which is all about achieving your full potential and becoming the best version of who you are.

Most of the time, my clients are fixated on this space. That's why they come to me. They want to be their best and fullest selves. So once they know their purpose, they stop at how it can shape their lives. But living a life of consequence is really about the highest level of Maslow's hierarchy of needs. That's where total lasting fulfillment resides and where I'm inviting you to set your sights. You need to break through self-actualization to self-transcendence. That means living above and beyond yourself for something higher.

I bring this up because women tend to tank here in the life-planning process. They want to figure out their life purpose so they can build a happy life only for themselves. And that's great. You deserve to be happy. But your individual happiness is not a compelling enough reason to live. Test me on this. I can testify that, having transitioned from an insecure and disempowered adolescent to a thriving woman, success wasn't enough to satisfy me. I got the body I wanted, married the love of my life, built a seven-figure business, purchased my dream home, and had the most amazing kid. It's not enough. The most meaningful part of my life continues to be stewarding all I have for others to flourish. It's living beyond myself that gives life purpose. I see the same being true for my clients all the time.

Inevitably the women who come back to me bored and dissatisfied years after discovering their purpose are the women who viewed their purpose as a framework for self-service. So I'm throwing this in now for you at the start of our journey together: As we explore your life purpose through the coming chapters, leave room to live for something greater than yourself.

THE GOOD LIFE

In Jeremiah 29, God told his people how to thrive on this side of heaven. In some ways you could say God was painting the ultimate vision for the good life. He encouraged them to build a life, even though they were in a foreign land. He said settle down and be free to grow families that increase in number. But ultimately he threw in the command to "seek the peace and prosperity of the city . . . because if it prospers, you too will prosper."[3]

You are an immovable force in the water. You are created to stand tall, establish roots, and flourish. But the secret to your fulfillment is to live beyond yourself for the flourishing of all those who surround you. Be sure that your life purpose keeps you seeking the peace and prosperity of others because *there* you will find meaning.

Are you ready to unlock the mystery of your version of the good life? As Dolly Parton said, "Find out who you are and do it on purpose."[4] Let's do that. We're going to pan through your life for the golden parts of your identity as we work through the next section. Remember to view each activity or challenge as an opportunity to enhance your vision so your heart can lean into becoming who you are.

Let's begin by examining what you do exceedingly well. Get ready to explore the realm of your talents.

seven

THE IMPORTANCE OF KNOWING YOUR TALENTS

What people think about you
means nothing in comparison to
what you believe about yourself.

SHAUNA NIEQUIST, *PRESENT OVER PERFECT*

Before we dive into talents and illuminate what you do well, can we acknowledge who God says you are?

Fair warning: I'm about to get super "churchy" on you. Picture me wearing my Sunday best with a big hat and patent leather heels if you need a visual. But spare me the eye rolls for a second. I need to go "full women's ministry" on you because who you think you are informs how you might receive what I plan to say about talents.

YOUR IDENTITY IN CHRIST

Please forgive the detour, but let's take a look at how God describes you in the following verses:*

- You are complete (Ps. 23:1).
- You are blameless (Col. 1:22).
- You are sanctified (Heb. 2:11).
- You are a member of a royal priesthood (1 Peter 2:9–10).
- You are loved (1 John 4:10).
- You are accepted (Rom. 15:7).
- You are free (Rom. 6:18).
- You are God's workmanship (Eph. 2:10).
- You are protected (Ps. 91:14).
- You are redeemed (Rev. 5:9).
- You are valuable (1 Cor. 6:20).
- You are chosen (Col. 3:12 and 1 Thess. 1:4).
- You are like Christ (1 John 4:17).
- You are firmly rooted and being built up by Christ (Col. 2:7).
- You are the fragrance of God to the world around you (2 Cor. 2:15).
- You are bold (2 Cor. 3:12).
- You are wonderfully made (Ps. 139:14).
- You are more than a conqueror (Rom. 8:37).
- You are brand-new (2 Cor. 5:17).

These are just a handful of things we find in the Bible about who God says you are.

---

* Bonus Bible points if you look up and read the actual passages in context.

Keep these declarations over your identity top of mind. We're about to spend the next several pages talking about talents, and I don't want you to overinflate the importance of *what* you do by disregarding *who* you are. Those are separate things, remember? You are not what you do, because you are a who, not a what.

You are a daughter of a King. Full stop. That is your first and most important identity. And in addition to that royal heritage, you have been gifted with a special set of skills—not unlike Liam Neeson in *Taken*. These gifts are how people see you show up as your best self in the world. We call them talents, and your talents allow you not only to flourish personally but also to make your greatest impact. But your talents are not equivalent to your identity; they are only a part of it.

By now I hope you've internalized that you are wildly complex and multifaceted. You cannot be reduced to a handful of activities. It's important that you hold on to this difference between your *being* and your *doing* so as not to fall back into the significance trap yet again. I'm giving you this heads-up because there will come a moment toward the close of this book when I'm going to encourage you to put your talents to use. And as you exercise your talents, the temptation will be to get caught up in the performance of your own gifting, leading you back into the significance struggle. Don't drink your own Kool-Aid, as the saying goes. Hold on to the fact that you have immeasurable value before you ever lift a finger or step out into the world.

With that said, over the next several pages, I want to help you put language to your talents so you can more easily describe how you operate in the world—and further, help you access their power. Remember how I said in the last chapter that your life purpose lies at the intersection of your talents, heart, and influence? Those are the coordinates for a purposeful life. Discovering your talents is the first stop on your path to purpose.

I am going to throw a ton of exercises at you throughout the remainder of this chapter and the next so you can assess what you do from different angles. It might feel like we're covering the same ground again and again, but repetition is important. In order to find your talents, we need to see how they consistently appear across different spheres of your life so you can have confidence that the information you're gaining is accurate. But first let's define what talents are.

WHAT ARE TALENTS?

A talent is something you do exceedingly well and that brings you a great sense of relief, exhilaration, and/or satisfaction to do. It's an action you take in your "Zone of Genius" (to borrow the language of psychologist Gay Hendricks). In this zone, you demonstrate more than competence or excellence, doing only what you are "uniquely suited to do."[1]

Because of this select nature of talents, we each have just a handful to possess as our own. (Think two to five instead of ten or twenty.) I use the word *possess* with hesitation, because the women I work with rarely describe their talents as something they own. More often they allude to talent as a power that possesses them or a strength they feel a compulsion to use. You may experience this sensation as well, feeling called or lured to exercise a small number of gifts again and again to your great delight. Hendricks similarly describes being drawn toward our genius, writing, "Your Zone of Genius beckons you with increasingly strong calls as you go through your life."[2] In this way, talents can feel otherworldly as you wield them, like genius passing through you to accomplish its own purpose, with you as the medium.

This is starting to sound a little woo-woo (I hear it too), but stick with me. I promise not to go full Gwyneth on you.[†] But I want you to grasp that there is a supernatural element to your talents. In *Year of Yes*, Golden Globe–winning television producer and screenwriter Shonda Rhimes described her talent for writing. Though in general Rhimes said writing for television is akin to laying track for a moving train—fast-paced and high-pressure— hear how she personally experienced her craft.

> I call it the *hum*. There's a hum that happens inside my head when I hit a certain writing rhythm, a certain speed. When laying track goes from feeling like climbing a mountain on my hands and knees to feeling like flying effortlessly through the air. Like breaking the sound barrier. Everything inside me just shifts. I break the writing barrier. And the feeling of laying track changes, transforms, shifts from exertion into exultation.[3]

This otherworldliness is a key distinction from all the other personality stuff you've learned through the years, such as the color of your parachute or a DISC assessment—because, on the one hand, your talents are concrete and measurable. You can understand them, describe them, and witness them at work. In some cases, your talents might even feel so natural or inherent to who you are that you may not even think to mention them.

[†] One of my best friends wanted me to note that this is my second shot at Gwyneth in this book, and we're only halfway through it. What is my beef? #LOL If Ms. Paltrow ever reads this, I hope she knows I love her work, and it's nothing personal.

And yet there is a holy quality to the exercise of your talents. They are literally gifts God has deposited in you that you are meant to steward for the good of others. In this way, they are *more than* strengths or great skills. As you employ them, grace goes before you. This is a telltale sign of a talent: The return on effort far outpaces the investment of energy you make at the start. Even when the work is hard, it feels so good.

In *Culture Making*, Andy Crouch described this kind of grace associated with calling. He referred to a "divine multiplication that far exceeds your efforts."[4] Crouch wrote, "When we undertake the work we believe to be our vocation [talents], we experience the joy and humility that come only when God multiplies our work so that it bears thirty, sixty, and a hundredfold beyond what we could expect from our feeble inputs."[5] That's why we can't quite categorize talents as skills or strengths, though they certainly encompass both. They are better described as access points where God most frequently works through you to accomplish a greater purpose beyond your finite intentions.

Now you may be thinking, *Chanel, that's a little much.* At least, that's what my clients say. They can accept the idea of skill, but the touch point of a divine finger in their lives? That feels far-fetched. That feels . . . other, like something that couldn't possibly describe their life story. Maybe it feels that way for you too. Perhaps upon reading this your heart is already echoing the words Marianne Williamson wrote long ago: "'Our deepest fear is that we are powerful beyond measure. It is our light, not our darkness that most frightens us.' We ask ourselves, Who am I to be brilliant, gorgeous, talented, fabulous?"[6]

You are the daughter of a King. Don't shrink from your high station. As we unpack your life story and allow your talents to rise to the top, you'll see how magnificent you really are. First, let me tell you about one of my favorite clients ever—my dear friend Blair.

Blair: How Talents Show Up

If you ever meet Blair, one of the first things you'll experience in her presence is that time immediately slows. Around Blair, clocks tick—and then get around to "tocking" when they feel like it. She has the ability to be insanely present in a way I haven't experienced with anyone else in my life. Even with three kids running around her ankles or dinner burning on the stove, beckoning for her attention, Blair's entire being exudes the message, *There is no place I'd rather be than here with you.* She is a walking place of respite.

So during our two-day intensive, I wasn't surprised when, after some wordsmithing, we landed on the language of "Moment Maker" and a "Curator of Rest" to describe two of Blair's talents. Her life story was punctuated by examples, time and again, of her uncanny ability to cultivate and curate moments that fostered deep soul rest in herself and others. Whether she was at home with her family, doing research abroad in Nepal, or participating in her local church community, focus and presence were given to the moment when Blair showed up.

And here's what was powerful about finding that language to describe her talents. All along, Blair just thought she was slow. She'd held on to an insecurity that she couldn't move, speak, or think fast enough to keep up with what people wanted. Living in New York City only magnified this lie of inadequacy, as she rushed about the city keeping pace with the Big Apple rhythm. Even though she held her own in the city, she felt an internal dissonance that life was not moving at the right velocity. And beyond speed, Blair feared that she made too much of everything, collecting little trinkets and baubles to fill her space in order to create the perfect moment. Was she too much? Was she not enough?

In the analysis of her talent space, we saw how grace went before her as she warmly invited people to step out of hurried rhythms and to experience rest alongside her. Simple moments (to her), such as putting out a pot of tea or handing someone a throw blanket to cozy up and rest, brought exponential peace to the recipient of her kindness. Blair's home was a space where people could relax and be themselves. The more she leaned into her "quirks" as talents and saw her power for what it was, the more impact she started to have. Shortly after her life-planning session, she started a candle company called Brown Fox Collective where she and a partner sold specialty mixed and hand-poured soy candles. Talk about curating moments of rest.[‡]

Finding My Talent

I'll give you another example from my own life. When I was in college, I used to travel down to Orange County from Los Angeles to attend a weekly college ministry at Saddleback Church. This was back in the day when Pastor Rick Warren's church was just coming into its fullness as a megachurch. To be honest, I hated the huge scene on Sundays; I'd grown up at Saddleback and remembered the days of meeting in high school gyms or when Rick and Kay came by our home personally to drop off groceries when my mom was struggling with money. I missed the personal connection that inevitably dissipates as a

---

‡ Fun fact: Blair's slow, whimsical hand lettering graces the cover of this book. I let out an audible sigh of relief whenever I see it.

church grows. But I loved the intimacy of our small college ministry. With its moody low lights in a small tent in the parking lot, it had what the kids call "a vibe." I made a point to be there every Thursday night.

At some point, I started serving in the community by typing up a recap of whatever the message was so it could be included as a devotional in the weekly college e-newsletter. I'd synthesize what the pastor said at the service, find a winsome way to expand on the content, and throw in a few prompts to inspire study or action throughout the week. It took me about an hour, and I loved helping, so I didn't think much of it.

But then a funny thing started to happen. My friends who received the emails kept telling me how much they loved them. They'd say the sermons were great but the points were really driven home by my devotions. I'd hear time and again other students saying, "I never thought of it that way." Then things got really weird. Some folks on the mailing list started sharing them with people outside the college ministry. My best friend told me she sent a copy to her mom, who then forwarded it on to people she knew overseas. Soon I was hearing that people all over the world—people I didn't know and who were disconnected from our church—were reading these little messages I wrote. The newsletter had legs. Something bigger than me was at play.

What I learned was that I had a way of putting language to what people were thinking and feeling in a way that made them feel understood. And I could synthesize the breadth of wisdom I'd gleaned from a source and apply it like a balm to the specific areas where people were hurting. Writing the devotions felt like dipping into my secret sauce, and the formula was synthesis + insight + catalyzation = powerful content.

At the time it didn't feel so powerful; I thought I was just doing my thing. But these were the telltale signs of a talent at work. The return was greater than the investment of effort, people were blessed by my actions, and I felt compelled to do it because it brought me tremendous peace and joy, like I was dancing around in my own skin. It wasn't until years later that I named being an Insight Communicator as one of my core talents. I also identified a talent as a Transformation Facilitator[§] who instigates change and growth in others.

So that's what a talent is like. It's something you do exceedingly well, that may feel like a little—but not a lot—of effort. Sometimes you do it on purpose, and other times without thinking. But whenever you use your talent, you come alive to the moment and others take note.

THE IMPORTANCE OF KNOWING YOUR TALENTS

I want to help you find your core talents, because I know every woman has them. Sometimes they are traits you've ignored, overlooked, or dismissed, but they are the beginning of your larger purpose in the world. Even if they are hidden, trust that they exist. Do any possible talents come to mind?

[§] By the way, you didn't miss anything. There is no master list of talents for you to draw from and use as your own. Each talent I've described here, for myself or my clients, is something custom we develop in the life-planning process. We look at all the gathered information, and after staring at it until our eyes get blurry like second graders looking at a Magic Eye image, the talents become detectable. When you grab your talent language later in chapter 8, you'll see what I mean. Don't stress about it. When you get to that point, do your best to find words that are meaningful to you, and keep a thesaurus handy so you can use more colorful language where possible.

If you said not really, you're not alone. It's staggering how many women are unable to succinctly articulate what they do well. A 2019 market research study found that the self-improvement world is an $11 billion industry with expectations for it to reach $13 billion by 2023. To put that in perspective, that's enough money to buy the entire population on the continent of Africa a copy of Jen Sincero's *You Are a Badass*. And get this: Women make up 70 percent of the consumers of this booming self-help market.[7] In spite of all that spending, I find that when you ask women to brag about themselves or even describe what they do in the world, most women stutter and stammer. Huh?

This is not okay with me, and I hope it's not okay with you either. Because when we don't know our talents or when we're unable to wrap language around them, there are real consequences. Some are hard to quantify, like insecurity and lack of confidence. Constantly operating outside your gifting can leave you feeling like you have nothing of real value to give to others, or it can deplete your resources as you pull from reserves of skill you don't actually have. Comparison rears its ugly head, and you can find it hard to distinguish yourself from others without language to differentiate how you show up compared to the woman next to you.

Other consequences take years to notice, such as burnout and exhaustion. Because when you don't know your talents, you can waste time and energy on low-level actions that are not within your sweet spot. You start to feel stuck or lost at sea. So many of my clients come into care complaining about the energy drain from analysis paralysis. One woman I worked with said, "Chanel, I know I'm theoretically good at a lot of things. Praise God for that! I just don't know what I'm *really* good at, so I keep gravitating toward whatever feels safest. I am stuck. And I'm tired of feeling this way. I don't even have the energy to make a life change. I feel like I can't get out of this mental spiral."

Let's stop spiraling today because you deserve better. Go back and read that list of who you are at the start of the chapter if you've forgotten. You're royalty! Your contribution matters. Your actions have weight in the world. You deserve to state who you are and what you do, and then demand people put some respect on your name when they say it.

I'm going hard on this because I see too many women sitting on the sidelines of life because they don't know what they do outside of the roles they've been handed by others. Or worse, they *do* know what they do, but they've decided it's inadequate, unworthy, or inconsequential. And it's not their fault! The more I work with women, the more grieved I have become by the ways in which women are enculturated to play small.

Case in point: I once led a group coaching session for a collective of ambitious women who wanted to get activated in their life purpose. As they went around the circle sharing their experiences, one woman explained that while she had big dreams and had accomplished quite a bit, she'd never been given the message that her purpose mattered. This, by the way, was a woman with an MBA who had risen through the ranks in a male-dominated industry. She described how her whole life she'd been taught to shape-shift and take up minimal space in order to protect the male ego. Following her admission of what had been holding her back, woman after woman admitted the same. I was flummoxed, so I got curious and started asking other clients outside of the group. Most reported the same experience. In their spheres of influence, women weren't allowed to loom large enough to ever cast a shadow over the men. I don't know how that sits with you, but it makes me want to throw something.

So forgive me if I'm harping on this, but I have to speak up about how women are encouraged to play small—even if that means a little tugging at the hem of male patriarchy. But it's not just my clients. I've sat in too many rooms where I'm either the only female, or one of few, and watched as the talents of women were dissed and dismissed as lesser gifts. And I've seen too many instances of men taking credit for what women have done or created simply because women aren't taught to grandstand or declare how they are excelling. I can't keep watching my clients' spirits die.

We lose out on the full appreciation of God's power and provision in the world when we ignore or diminish the contribution women make. I think of Lydia of Thyatira from the book of Acts, who juggled a successful cloth business and still made time to use her talent for hospitality while facilitating the salvation of her entire household.[8] I think of clever Esther with her talent for tact and humble persuasion, who was positioned to exercise her influence to save an entire people group.[9] When we devalue women's talents, we miss the full extent of God's movement throughout the world. Let's not do that.

That's why this matters. Look, I care about you fully knowing your talents so you can color in some of the details about how you'll live out your version of the good life. But this is bigger than you. When you embrace your individual talents, you help set a collective standard for how all women are viewed in society. Your self-assertion has a ripple effect.

So let's normalize women boasting about their talents. Men do it all the time. It's not a character flaw. Try bragging about yourself for a minute. Imagine it's just the two of us sitting across from one another at your favorite Mexican restaurant toasting one another's recent successes over a couple of margaritas. What would we be celebrating in your life that you've done well? Say it out loud: "I just nailed it when I . . ."

Doesn't that feel good? Woo-sah!

WHAT KEEPS YOU OUT OF THE ZONE

Aside from the limits placed on us to play small, I wanted to note a few other obstacles that can hold women back from discovering or using their talents. Because maybe you're not completely in the dark on this, and you've already made a posterboard to bring to my rally mobilizing women to assert their value. You're #teamtalent but still feel stuck. If you're struggling to get activated in your talents, something else could be blocking you.

I find that many women stay out of their Zone of Genius or allow their talents to atrophy from perpetual neglect for the following reasons. See if any of these have become obstacles to finding your talents:

- **INERTIA:** It's easier to do what you've always done. Many women never tap into their talents because they are comfortable where they are. Far too easily pleased, maybe you're willing "to go on making mud pies in a slum," as C. S. Lewis wrote, because you cannot imagine a vacation by the sea.[10]
- **AFFIRMATION:** You might be addicted to your current recognition. Maybe you've come to do a handful of things

well—not exceedingly well, but good enough. And others have come to appreciate or rely on you for these abilities, often giving you praise or expressions of affirmation. You know you're made for more, but you can't imagine letting go of all the good you already have.

- **LACK OF AGENCY:** You've relinquished control of your life. At some point you started telling yourself a story that someone else is responsible for your life circumstances. You face life as a victim, powerless to change what you don't like.

- **FOCUS ON MONEY:** You know you possess a talent for something, but you can't figure out how to monetize it. So you're hesitating to step further into your talent because you're fixated on the idea of it bringing you personal profit. You devote your time to whatever makes money, even if it doesn't allow you to use your talents or make your unique impact in the world.

- **BURNOUT:** Your energy is so depleted from working outside of your genius space that you have no margin to put toward growing your talents. You feel like you're operating on empty, and trying to find avenues of self-care occupies your time. You'd like to know your talents, but you're too exhausted from the scorched earth beneath you.

- **PAST WOUNDS:** You tried to use your talents once, but you were mistreated or abused in the process. The sting of that past hurt accompanies any effort you make toward stepping out and using your talents now. You're stuck beneath a shame label someone slapped on you years ago, or you're stalled behind a wall of emotional pain.

- **SURVIVAL:** You have urgent matters to attend to in order to stay alive. Yeah, it would be nice to step into your talents, but you're focused on addressing your core needs. There is no shame in this, but it's a reality you're having to contend with as you also long to do what God created you to do.

Have any of these barriers kept you blocked from knowing what you do well? If so, I invite you to name the barrier, and then for a moment, set it aside so you can consider your talents without its influence. You have something to offer, and we need you, sis. Because in case you haven't noticed, things are looking pretty bleak out here in these streets. But I am confident that you have something meaningful to add to the world. Like Esther, you have been equipped "for such a time as this" to have impact.[11]

If you feel stuck, let me help you out a bit. Talents can feel elusive, and you may be thinking, *Chanel, I have no idea what my talents are because I do absolutely nothing well.* Or maybe you have the opposite problem. You're thinking, *I'm a jill-of-all-trades. I am struggling to narrow down what my true talents are.* I hear you. We are living in the age of the dilettante, where everyone does a little of this and a little of that. Regardless of which camp you're in now, I want to help you put language to your talents so we can start seeing how you're giving shape to the river of culture as it flows past you.

Blair is helping people slow down a bit.

I'm helping synthesize insights.

And you're doing . . .

Well, let's figure that out now. I want to walk you through how to discover your unique talents.

eight

HOW TO FIND YOUR FLICKERS OF GENIUS

The universe buries strange jewels deep within us
all, and then stands back to see if we can find them.

ELIZABETH GILBERT, *BIG MAGIC*

Naming your talents is more of an art than a science—which is a sophisticated way of saying, "I have no idea how to tell you the right way to do it."

Okay, wait, don't put down the book yet. I'm just trying to communicate that while I can give you all the steps (and I will in this chapter), there is something that happens with wordsmithing where you may need outside help. Particularly if you're a very concrete or literal thinker, you might struggle with naming your own talents. Or if commitment makes you uncomfortable, you might be afraid of putting yourself in a box. Where are all my S or P types on the Myers-Briggs Type Indicator? I'm looking at you. So don't get discouraged if you try the following and then get stuck. It doesn't mean you don't have talents. You just need a little support from an abstract thinker in your life to pull it all together. Enlist some help from a friend, life planner, or trusted listener who can wade through this with you.

Here's how you get started.

To find your talents, you'll need to look for a few clues. I call these clues *flickers of genius* because they kind of flit past us with a little gleam of what you do well. You can find these flickers all over the place, but here are some specific places I encourage you to look. Explore each of the following five areas, and jot down in a notebook any little flicker you might notice from that exercise. The more detail, the better. Make it visual with cutout images from magazines if that helps you. Or create a virtual mood board on Pinterest if that floats your boat. Just make sure to capture the flickers as you go.

Pro tip: You might want to use your Reclaim the Morning time to gradually work through and reflect on your flickers of genius. It's a great quiet space to process what you're learning about yourself.

#1: YOUR SELF-CONCEPT

Before you allow anything or anyone else to define who you are or what you do well, I want you to get some perspective on your own. How you see yourself is important, and your emotional response to the list of questions I'm going to ask you now can be very illuminating. As you go through the list, notice where your heart quickens. Which questions give you discomfort? Which questions energize you? Do any of the following questions trigger excitement or insecurity? At this stage, don't judge; just observe. Your reactions are all helpful bits of knowledge to glean. Become an expert at noticing not just the content of your thoughts but also your emotional response to the content.

Here are some questions to explore about how you see yourself:

- What have you done or experienced in the past that you are most proud of?
- What do you love to do?
- Where does your mind naturally drift when you're not focused on a particular subject?
- What can you get lost doing when you lose track of time or space?
- What makes something worthwhile for you?
- What does your heart most long for out of life?
- What motivates you (for better or worse) to take action?
- What do you need most in life?
- What do you wish to see in the world?
- What do you expect to happen within your lifetime?

Your responses to these questions provide a great baseline, as they may provoke flickers of what might be talents in your life to reveal themselves. Most of your passions, drives, needs, and hopes likely fall in line with your innate talents. Review your answers and highlight any common threads you see. Then explore some of these additional tools to help you gain more insight.

#2: MYERS-BRIGGS TYPE INDICATOR (MBTI)

You've probably heard about the Myers-Briggs Type Indicator at some point in your search for insight about how you're wired.

The MBTI was created by Isabel Briggs Myers and her mother, Katharine Briggs, as an instrument to help people identify their preferred way of engaging the world. Their instrument was based on the work of psychiatrist Carl Jung and his theory of personality. In the psychology world, the reliability of this tool is viewed as hit or miss. But it's a fantastic starting point even if it only helps you to begin collecting language that resonates with how you believe you operate in the world.

In this theory, there are four primary psychological preferences—sensation, intuition, feeling, and thinking. Through a short assessment, you'll learn if you're introverted or extroverted, sensing or intuitive, thinking or feeling, and judging or perceiving.* Based on your results, you'll come up with a four-letter description for your type. These sixteen types (the number of combinations from the eight letters) are often accompanied by a descriptive name that captures the essence of how you're wired. For example, I'm an INTJ, which is often called "The Architect" or "The Perfectionist." Rumor has it Michelle Obama is also an INTJ, so I'm not mad about it.

Take the assessment, and then note any flickers you see. What about your type most resonates with you? In reading the descriptions of this type, what do they commonly say you do well, or what do they point to as potential areas of skill? What kind of contribution do you imagine this personality type might make to solving a problem if she was sitting in a group of people?

---

* By the way, there are some free versions of this assessment online, such as at 16personalities.com. These assessments are not official, so don't @ me if you find the results aren't as spot-on as you'd like. I suggest making the fifty-dollar investment to take the real test at mbtionline.com because you'll get a wealth of resources along with it.

#3: THE ENNEAGRAM

Next up is to learn more about your Enneagram type. Knowing your Enneagram number is all the rage right now, particularly in Christian circles because of the framework's mystic origins. I'm an Enneagram type one, if you're curious, which is known as the Reformer or the Perfectionist (both accurate titles). Notice the common thread already with my Myers-Briggs type.

The Enneagram is a system of personality typing that describes patterns of how people interpret the world, manage emotions, and relate to others. If you take an Enneagram assessment, you'll find that you fall into one of the nine types, but I always recommend reading all the descriptions and deciding which type best describes you beyond just doing an assessment. In addition to your primary number, you can also discover your wing, which helps add some nuance to how you express your number.

A great place to start is reading *The Enneagram: A Christian Perspective* by Richard Rohr and then maybe hop around to other popular books like *The Road Back to You* by Ian Morgan Cron and Suzanne Stabile. Another option is to follow one of the five billion Instagram accounts dedicated to this system of personality typing.[†]

A quick word of caution: Hold the Enneagram loosely. I don't know what it is about this particular assessment, but people tend to become obsessed, speaking in Enneagram lingo all the time. Aside from that being . . . well, annoying, like speaking Christianese (which, for the record, is a very Enneagram one thing for me to say), it can quickly turn into a weapon used to

---

† Okay, five billion might be an exaggeration, but you have a lot of options.

critique all of someone's negative traits. If the Enneagram is not moving you toward compassion and grace for yourself and others, drop it like a hot potato.

If you can manage to cull insight from the Enneagram without becoming a fanatic, learn your type and then weed through the descriptions to pull any traits that might be flickers of your genius. For example, a quick read of an Enneagram one will tell you that I'm probably hyperinvested in living missionally, having integrity, and serving others. At my healthiest, as a one with a two wing (1w2), I am inspirational and hopeful, catalyzing others into action. These are great glimmers of potential talent. So I would write down that my talents likely involve me being purposeful, insightful, and service-oriented. What glimmers do you see in your type? Write them down now.

#4: CLIFTONSTRENGTHS

Over twenty-five million people use the CliftonStrengths Online Talent Assessment to thrive in work and life by leaning into their strengths instead of focusing on growing in their weaknesses. The StrengthsFinder helps you learn what you naturally do best among the thirty-four CliftonStrengths themes. According to Gallup, the organization behind CliftonStrengths, we all demonstrate competency in one or more of four domains: executing, influencing, relationship building, and strategic thinking. Once you take the assessment, you can find your top five strengths.

I have found this framework to be like one of those matryoshka sets—you know, those little Russian nesting dolls? I keep unpacking my strengths, and just when I think I've gotten to the bottom of insight, there is another little nugget of wisdom inside that I can investigate. One helpful way to examine your strengths for flickers of genius is to look at your top five strength themes and see how they manifest in your life. For example, my top five strengths are Individualization, Connectedness, Relator, Ideation, and Activator. When I read about these themes, I notice how I tend to see what's special or unique about each thing I encounter, but I also see connections between things. This might indicate a talent for pulling disparate items into systems. My ability to relate well to people might help my strength of activation, meaning I may be good at encouraging people to feel safe enough with me to break through inertia to make changes. I'm pretty aware of my talents by now, but it's fun to go back and see how my strengths give me little flickers of my talents at work.

What are your top five strengths? Write down any connections between the different themes and grab any language from the descriptions that jumps out at you. Pay attention to which strength domains are more heavily represented, as your talents will likely fall along similar lines. Jot down any notes and then head into the next exercise.

#5: FRIENDS AND FAMILY

Lastly, I want you to look for some outside input that might either expand or affirm talents you already suspect exist. It can also be valuable to get external feedback to combat one hurdle of the human ego. Our tendency is to self-deceive or overemphasize parts of ourselves that we'd like to believe are true (rather than what's actually true). I can't tell you the number of women who work with me one-on-one and start off the process claiming they are good at a particular thing we later find isn't true. They might say something like, "Chanel, I'm a natural leader." But when we dig into their life story, they have no evidence of ever leading anything. It turns out leadership is an aspirational talent, not an experienced talent.

Don't make that mistake. Collect evidence of your talents by getting validation from people in your life. Choose five to ten people you know whose opinion you value. It's best if you pull from different parts of your life to get a variety of perspectives. Include a mix of family members, colleagues, mentors, friends, and trusted acquaintances. It's natural to behave differently with different types of people because everyone draws out different aspects of our personality. Ask each person to name three qualities they would use to describe you. Then grab a tissue box, because if your loved ones are anything like mine, they will likely say the loveliest, most life-affirming statements about you that you've ever heard.

Track the responses and highlight any repeated themes to add to your list of flickers of genius. Once you have this info, we're ready to start pulling things together.

UNLOCKING YOUR GENIUS

Now that you have a ton of perspective about yourself, we need to do something with this information. The goal is to begin drawing conclusions about what you do when you're at your best. That means taking our analysis a step further. If you just leave all this insight on the page without applying it to reality in any constructive way, you've wasted your energy. You don't need more head knowledge. Your life is calling for wise, discerning action.

Here's how you stop the rumination. First, review all of what you've learned. Next, create a list of about five common threads you see. Out of all that information, what do you tend to do in life . . . like, a lot? Think across all life buckets (self, relationships, career, spirituality, and global engagement). What kind of activity do you see habitually showing up in your flickers of genius? Try to narrow each thread to one word so you have large overarching categories of activity. For example, you might see a theme of communication or perhaps advocacy. Maybe there is something about organizing or leading. What common threads of action are evident from your self-study?

Once you have your threads, you have unlocked your genius. These big categories will provide the foundation of your list of core talents. If you're feeling anxious about narrowing down your list too much or leaving something you care about behind, remember what we talked about with your Zone of Genius. We're trying to focus on what you do *exceedingly* well, and that should only be a handful of things. This is a space where less is more. Since we're trying to focus on how God moves through you in your life, if we capture a long laundry list of things you do well, we're likely to end up with a bunch of competencies or strengths. So don't inflate the number of threads. When I work with a client, I aim for two to five threads and err on the low side whenever possible. Often, I find that threads can be combined when I look a little deeper and see the driving action or genius behind the action. For example, someone might seem like they are a great communicator *and* a great planner. But when I look deeper, maybe there is a larger umbrella to explain these two, such as being a Vision Caster. The same might be true for you. Be ruthless in your editing.

FIND YOUR FLAIR

Once you have this basic list of talents, we want to level up a bit so this information can be most useful to you. We're going to do that by finding your flair.

Have you ever seen the movie *Office Space* with Jennifer Aniston? If not, set this book down right now and go watch it because it's hilarious and you need laughter in your life. In the movie, Aniston's character is named Joanna, and she works at what's meant to be a TGI Fridays–style restaurant. She wears the requisite uniform but gets reprimanded by her manager for the lack of "flair" on her suspenders—flair being the little buttons or pins intended to add character to the employee uniform. Joanna wears fifteen pieces of flair, which we learn is the company's bare minimum. Her manager encourages her to take it up a notch. He says, "Now, if you feel that the bare minimum is enough . . . okay. But some people choose to wear more, and we encourage that. You do want to express yourself?"[1]

Why am I telling you this? Aside from wanting to take any opportunity to quote *Office Space* to you, I bring it up because, right now, you're Jennifer Aniston's character, and I'm the manager. You've done the bare minimum by discovering your talent categories, but you need some more flair. I want you to consider *how* you use your talents so you can distinguish yourself from the woman standing next to you. You can do this by adding a qualitative aspect to your talents.

Here's an example. One of my talents is problem-solving. If you were looking over my shoulder as I walked through the earlier exercises, you'd see how I pulled a common thread of problem-solving from the flickers of genius all over my notebook. But problem-solving isn't special. Lots of women do that. We want to know *how* I problem-solve differently from someone else. What's my flair?

If I sat with that question a little longer, I'd notice that I hate solving surface-level problems. I'm unmotivated to help you find quick solutions or make minuscule changes. To me that feels like rearranging deck chairs on the *Titanic*. My approach is to always get to the core problem, because I believe if we don't dig, we'll keep encountering the same issue time and again. Problems are like weeds; we have to pull them out at the root. So if I were to find my flair around problem-solving, I would use more interesting language to describe this talent. I'm not just a problem-solver; I am a Core Solutionist.

Okay, back to you.

Grab the common threads you gleaned from unlocking your genius. For each thread, attach a qualifier to the action. If you're a leader, what kind of leader are you, or how do you lead? If you're an advocate, who or what do you advocate for, or how do you approach it? The qualities and characteristics you captured from friends and family are likely good sources of information about how you do things because others pick up your unique style. Try to turn each thread into a noun (even if it sounds funny, because we're adults and we do what we want), and then pair it with a qualifier. You want to be able to say in a few words what each of your talents is and then have a longer description in mind.

Remember, my friend Blair is a Moment Maker. I am a Core Solutionist. Who are you?

USING YOUR TALENTS

Phew! We did it! Give yourself a pat on the back if you've been able to wade through all this information. If you still feel stuck, don't panic. Sit with the insight a little longer or enlist outside help. It's incredibly difficult to see yourself, and your view will only be as good as the mirror you have. Sometimes reading through exercises or journaling is not the best mirror for everyone's personality type. So don't beat yourself up if you're still asking questions. Find a better mirror that works for you. That might mean hiring a life planner‡ or verbalizing this with a trusted friend. Self-reflection may only get you so far, and that's okay. If you faithfully did the exercises in this chapter, at the very least you now know more about yourself than you may ever have considered in the past. That's progress!

You can do whatever you want with these talents now that you've done the work. Many of my clients revamp their résumés or use them to describe themselves in job interviews. Others build businesses where they create verticals around their talents, using them to guide the services offered. Some allow this information to help them say no to new opportunities that are outside of their talents or direct how they interact with family and friends. The options for how you use your talents are endless.

Can you believe we're only at the start of the process?

---

‡ Visit chaneldokun.com/lifestartsnow for recommendations on excellent life planners.

Knowing your talents is only the first step in unlocking your purpose. We have to get moving if we want to pull your head fully above water. The next step is to figure out where to put your talents to use. That requires us to move on to the second coordinate of your life purpose—your heart. Your activated heart will give us the direction we need so you're not throwing your pearls before swine. You've been specifically called to focus your talents in a certain area, and I want to help you find your sweet spot.

Let's explore the story God's been telling through your life, and turn on your passion.

nine

THE REDEMPTION OF YOUR LIFE STORY

The world is hungry for people to own their stories
and to create safe spaces for others to do the same.

ASHLEY ABERCROMBIE, *RISE OF THE TRUTH TELLER*

In all my years of study on purpose and vocation, I've come across countless definitions of calling. But my favorite comes from Frederick Buechner in his book *Wishful Thinking*. He says succinctly that God calls you to "the place where your deep gladness and the world's deep hunger meet."[1]

Well, we can all pack up and go home because he's nailed it, right? It's beautiful in its simplicity—so much weight embedded in one little sentence. I love his use of the word *gladness*. It captures the essence of joy and the kind of exhilaration I'm talking about experiencing when we use our talents. Gladness is grace going before you, where you get to delight in the pleasure of using the tools you've been given.

But what of the world's deep hunger? How could we possibly narrow down the prevalent need around us? So great is the depravity and brokenness in the world, we'd be crippled by a mere cursory survey. If we're to find your calling, to clarify your version of the good life God is calling you to live, we need to zoom in on the exact point of hunger you're meant to engage.

As I've sat with Buechner's framing and carried it into work with clients from all walks of life, I've come to find that an activated heart is the best guidepost for where to engage the world's hunger. Knowing what you care about in general is the clue to where you can serve specifically. Through decades of interactions, your heart has been molded to care about the world in a particular way. No one on the planet is just like you. Your heart is singular in its formation. Out of nearly eight billion people, no one shares an identical composite of experiences or ideals that inform how you view the world.

For some reason, women have trouble believing me when I say this. Maybe it's because I keep telling my clients they aren't unicorns that they have difficulty reconciling this idea. *Which is it? Am I unique or like everyone else?* But both things are true. Human beings have more in common than not, sharing many of the same fears and hopes for their individual lives. But your heart is the exception to that rule. You're an anomaly. Every woman I've worked with has been wired to care about the world in a different way, tripped up by unique irritations and grieved by different evils.

God's grace is that our hearts are not all sensitive to the same wounds. One woman I coached cared deeply about providing people with access to clean water. Another was fixated on saving the vulnerable from sex trafficking and protecting children from abuse. I've worked with a woman intent on breaking down gender biases and still another who considered the greatest problem in the world to be the lack of sustainable building materials. While we can all tacitly agree that these issues are important, our hearts are likely not moved at the same time to the same degree to focus on dismantling these cancers of the human experience. We care, and we would donate a few dollars to the cause or sign a petition. But our shared disappointment and passion disperse at the point of greater action.

I want to help you uncover the specific part of the world's deep hunger that you're drawn to address—the hunger that activates your heart. Your talents are waiting to be used, but we want to apply them in the location that sets your life on fire so you're excited to jump out of bed every morning. The circumstances you've walked through, the pain you've endured, and the dreams you hope to bring to life all sit in the recesses of your heart. And all those things reveal the little cracks in the matrix you've been designed to detect.

You see, your individual life journey has given you acute knowledge of issues and made you tender to aspects of the world that also grieve the one who created it. The things you care about? God cares about them, too, with an even greater understanding of their complexity. And therein lies the gladness. In that space of shared heartbreak with God, we get to channel our talents to participate in the renewal of all things. Tucked into the Bible in Matthew 25 is the parable of the talents. It's an object lesson in how God resources each person according to their ability, and he invites those who steward their talent well to be his partner. We get to be colaborers, using our God-given genius to redeem that which has been sullied and warped from its intended design.

I don't know about you, but that gets me excited. That makes me feel like my life matters. Screw significance. I want a life of consequence where I am stewarding the best of what I have to make the best of what already is. That feels deeply centering to me, like my head is coming out of the water and my feet are beginning to steady. With that level of focus, I can get my bearings and start to see where I'd like to go. I see how I can use my past to construct a better future. I hope you can too. I want you to have that level of clarity. What if you have lived a particular life and been handed tools you can use effectively for a reason?

So let's talk about your story so you can begin to add some why to what you do. To push forward in a meaningful life direction, we must go back to your personal history and unpack the pattern of how God has moved or spoken in your life to this point. I call this process redeeming your history.

REDEEMING YOUR HISTORY

Have you ever made sense of your personal story, pulling together all the fragments of your life into a comprehensive narrative? Maybe you've been living a million miles a minute and have never slowed down to pay attention to how you got where you're seated now. Or maybe your life is littered with painful events and experiences you'd rather not remember. To protect your sanity, maybe you have blocked out the past and tried to stay focused on the present and future. I hear that.

But can I encourage you that there is gold in your life story that can enrich your life if only you'd pause to notice? This isn't a possibility; it's a point of certainty. No matter how many women

I work with and how bleak their stories have been, I always find there is freedom to be culled from the events of the past. Understanding your history is worth your time and energy.

Maya Angelou once said, "The more you know of your history, the more liberated you are."[2] I believe she's right. I mean, Dr. Angelou was a genius—so she was almost always right. Wholeness matters. Individual moments can be meaningful and, upon reflection, speak partial truths to us. But the gravity of some moments can only be understood in context as the whole plotline unfolds. When we recount the full picture of how our lives have evolved, we no longer sit in bondage to outdated narratives. We are permitted to tell new, more complete stories of who we are that bring joy and relief.

Not only does redeeming your history free you, but it can also help you discern how God has uniquely called you through the years. As you retell your story, you can tap into what you have long since cared about at a gut level, beyond the fleeting fascinations that thrill you season to season. By facing your life story, you get to reach deep into the well of the woman you have always been to see how you were designed to engage the world.

In so doing, you will find your *life equity*—the term I use to describe the transcendent narrative threads that, woven together, form your story. Each experience you've gone through in your life has enabled you to accrue little shares of meaning and purpose that now amount to something of substance. For example, when you were able to thrive in spite of your parents' divorce, you built equity in resilience. The time you spent in the library during high school studying feverishly to pass the AP exam? That gave you shares of academic perseverance that you can now draw against.

The breakups and setbacks, the career twists and cross-country moves, have all given you equity in different spaces to guide your purpose.

How, you might ask?

It's simple. All of those experiences shaped your heart and inflamed your passion toward certain aspects of human life. When we pay attention to them and honor where you've been, these indicators help us nail down where your individual story connects to the larger story of humanity. In that space, we can begin channeling your talents for greater impact. Before I give you the specifics on how to capture your life equity, let me show you how this process worked with my client Tanya.

Tanya: How to Find Life Equity

When I first started working with Tanya, she was coming off a bad work transition. She'd been let go abruptly from a job where she was having considerable impact. But she was worried about what to do next because she couldn't discern if her life purpose was something similar to what she was doing in her previous job or wholly different. After years working in one sector, she couldn't see where she ended and the job began. We were able to get clear on her talents, but we couldn't figure out where she was meant to apply them. We needed to activate her authentic heart.

During her life-planning session, I asked Tanya to share her life story with me. Over a couple of hours, she shared tale after tale of everything from childhood trauma to starting a grassroots community service organization as a teenager before heading off to college. Her life post-college was marked by romantic trysts and a difficult breakup that left her longing to build a stable family life one day. We scanned back through her early life, recounting vivid memories of her parents' divorce, custody battles, and tense, sometimes violent moments shifting between households. We even revisited instances of sexual abuse when Tanya fell between the cracks, neglected by angry parents during her rebellious teenage years.

Resilient and hopeful, we watched how little Tanya seemed to "attract" friends and acquaintances who were also children of divorced families. Fast-forward to an adult Tanya, who was devoted to healing trauma through therapy and personal development. The chapters of her life spoke of the hardship of divorce, the vulnerability of girls in broken families, and the power of mental health care to protect.

By the time we arrived at her present-day life experiences, it was no surprise that she'd found meaning in work that supported protecting young girls from abuse and trauma. The chapters of her life were repeatedly centered on acknowledging the vulnerability of women and girls in broken families. That's what made her come alive, and you could see her light up the moment she talked about advocacy opportunities for children of divorce. That was her theme, her life equity.

CAPTURING YOUR LIFE EQUITY

Now it's your turn. Let's try a simple exercise. I say simple because it's straightforward, but it may not be easy to complete. I want you to practice telling your story. Consider it a kind of narrative therapy, because I want you to re-author your life. This is a subtle act of subversion. For as long as you can remember, your life has been defined by chasing after what the world says significance looks like. That's what caused you to start drowning. You were caught up in someone else's story. Often my clients will describe their discontent as feeling like a supporting actress in their own life. Have you ever felt that way? Are you an extra in your own story, sitting in the background with life just happening to you? It's time to reclaim the narrative and take back control of the life you've lived so you can operate from the inside out. That means locating the storehouses of meaning and purpose that have been with you all along but were hidden behind the urgency of daily priorities or shrouded by others' expectations.

Here's how to get started.

First, mark your moments.

Identify between ten and twenty catalytic life events that have shaped your story. Imagine you're sitting across from me over lunch telling me how you landed where you are now. As you go, pull out the key moments that impacted you. Write them down in a journal or type them up on your device so we can sit with them for a few minutes. Use that expert skill you've developed by getting curious about yourself and looking beyond the immediate content to see what truths may be lurking in the shadows.

By catalytic events, I don't mean the most traumatic things to ever have happened to you. And you certainly don't need to put together a highlight reel of your life. It's not always the major highs or tremendous lows that shape our identity. Small moments can have a massive impact. Catalytic events are those that propel your story forward and give nuance to your narrative. For example, here are types of events that have directed my clients' lives:

- Brooke attended an art school in New York at twenty years old.
- Allison had a pregnancy scare at thirty-one years old.
- Amy auditioned for the part of Annie at eleven years old.
- Lindsay heard about mission trips abroad for the first time in a school chapel service when she was twenty-two years old.

These seemingly minor (and sometimes major) events pushed their stories along to lead them into the life they have now. I'll give you an example of a catalytic event from my life.

One of my earliest memories is teaching myself how to read when I was four years old. For months I was obsessed with the story of *Cinderella* and asked my mom to read it to me nightly until she finally refused. I can still remember my tiny hands holding my big pink board book and thinking, *Well, fine. I'll do it myself.* Defiant and unwavering, I pieced the words on the page together with what I had memorized until I could read the full story on my own. Then I extended my reading skill to other books until it was clear I could read almost anything off the bookshelf, even before hitting kindergarten. In the larger scheme of things, this isn't the most pivotal life event anyone has ever had. But in the context of my story, it's incredibly catalytic. I've had greater traumas (such as losing my mom just before my wedding day) or greater joys (such as studying abroad in London for a semester). But teaching myself to read was noteworthy because it crystallized at a young age what I still believe to be true about myself now. I decided then I wouldn't let other people determine what I was capable of. And I learned that if I didn't know how to do something, I could teach myself. What are your catalytic events?

Imagine you're writing a memoir. Write down the situations or occurrences that moved you—the main character—and your plotline along, whether they be big or small happenings. Consider all five of the life buckets (self, relationships, career, spirituality, and global engagement) so you have a 360-degree view of your experience. Beginning with your childhood until you reach the present day, work your way through the stages of life by exploring what happened throughout each season that shaped who you are.

As I cautioned with talents, I encourage you to be ruthless in your editing so you don't have too much content to sift through later. I find that the average forty-year-old woman has between twelve and fifteen catalytic events to capture, so use that as a gauge for where you might land in terms of quantity.

Next, label your lessons.

Once you have collected your different catalytic events, assign a label to each that describes the redemptive lesson you learned from that moment. The key word here is *redemptive*. I'm not asking you to sugarcoat the things that have happened to you. I'm trained as a therapist, remember? I like to call a spade a spade, so this isn't intended to dismiss the weight of your past. I don't ever want to be in the business of devaluing trauma or undermining the significance of negative experiences. But I have found that God can use all circumstances for good even when they were intended for harm—including terrible situations like abuse. The trauma itself is bad. No question or gray when it comes to that. Furthermore, the woman you are in light of all past wounds or mistakes is valuable and redeemed.

When certain events happened to you in the past, you may not have been able to decide the meaning of them at the time. The full value of the experience may have taken years to appreciate. But now, with hindsight, you have the power to process and rewrite the life you've lived. And if you get to retell the story, why not retell it with hope? Snap those suspenders, Jennifer Aniston, and add a little flair!

Here's what it looks like to assign a redemptive label. Consider the specific experiences from your past and list them like chapters in a book. Then ask yourself how God might have used that moment to teach you something. What message did you take away from it? What truth did you learn about yourself, others, the world, or God as a direct result of that event? Or in what way did you live differently following that chapter of your life? Take your time processing. Revisiting our past can be inspiring, and it can also be painful. Be gentle with yourself and practice incredible self-care as you recount your life.

∽

Let me show you how I apply a redemptive label. I told you about how I started reading at age four. My label for that catalytic event: "You have the power to do it yourself." Another example of a catalytic event was at the age of fifteen, when my father passed away from cancer. We'd had a complicated relationship, and his death sent my family reeling. Overwhelmed by the loss of my dad and, soon after, the loss of my maternal grandmother, my mom began to make a series of really bad decisions for our well-being. Her mental and physical health started to decline, and I realized she was incapable of raising me. I needed to raise myself and serve as her caregiver. So when I was a teenager, we shifted roles, and I grew up faster than expected. There were many lessons to be learned during that time, but the redemptive message I took away from that season was that I didn't have to inherit the choices of my parents. I didn't have to live their same stories or repeat the mistakes I believed they'd made. And I could also maintain empathy for the series of circumstances that led them to make what I'd later call poor decisions. I title that chapter of my life "Honoring and releasing the pattern." My life has been characterized by this balance, where I continually see hardship and brokenness but trust in the possibility of something new.

Remember, we are going through this exercise because I want you to hunt for any pocket of untapped resources or direction in your life that might guide future action. Keep that intention at the top of your mind. The experiences we've lived and the truths that have changed us become our most powerful assets to impact those around us.

Because this is where you have expert knowledge. This is how God has softened your heart to care about something in the world you might otherwise not have noticed. What does your heart break for in the world? When you examine the collection of events that have most affected you, do you feel drawn to any part of the world's deep hunger? There are so many things to care about and so many problems to solve. Luckily you're not responsible for solving them all. You're only meant to influence the specific area for which God has given you expertise and passion. Find that space in your story. Where do you have life equity?

The story you're telling yourself about yourself is important. Your story has power. Author and narrative therapist Stephen Madigan wrote, "It is the stories people tell and hold about their lives that determine the meaning they give to their lives."[3] If you've been telling yourself a story of despair or disappointment, that's the meaning you will make of who you are. If you repeat a narrative that you are ordinary and nothing about you is interesting, that's exactly how you'll feel about yourself every day. But if you wake up tomorrow and start to tell yourself an alternative story—one where each experience has helped mold you into the woman you are today—you might start to hold your head a little higher.

I see this all the time with my clients. They don't think their life story is spectacular, but I make them each tell me their history in a complete narrative. As I did with Tanya, we sift through all the details to extract the catalytic events. As they outline the various experiences they've had, inevitably we land on a theme that seems to characterize who they are. By *theme*, I mean some place of hurt or brokenness in humanity they perpetually seem to be circling.

PULLING IT ALL TOGETHER

Once you have your chapters labeled, create the large sections of your life story. Do there seem to be any themes that have followed you throughout your life? If you were to step outside of yourself and look at your story objectively from a forty-thousand-foot view, what does it seem like the main character has cared about in her life? What issues or causes seem to repeatedly surface as she walks in and out of scenes? Does she appear to be particularly invested in solving any problem? What obstacle has she overcome, or what pain has she persevered through that might make her an expert guide for someone else going through a similar situation? That's your total life equity, and it's the sacred space where you're meant to apply your talents.

"At the intersection of grace and the cross," Andy Crouch wrote so beautifully, "is where we are called to dig into the dirt, cultivate and create."[4] In this holy space, where our hearts have come undone and learned to break in the same way Christ's heart was broken on the cross by the depravity of the world, we will find our purpose. We find our cause, our burden, and the world's deep need. That equity of hurt, or perhaps pain of the potential for goodness, that we have observed in a special area throughout our lives becomes a North Star—drawing us to give our genius to the renewal of what's dying.

I wonder how this exercise will strike you. I expect you'll have mixed emotions because returning to the past can be painful. I bet you'll hit upon a few past hurts along the way. And I wouldn't be much of a therapist if I didn't take a moment to draw your attention to some of these wounds you may graze as you walk through your life story.

But let's pause here for a moment. Go through the exercises, and then practice a little self-care to honor the hard work you've done already. In the next chapter we'll spend a little more time activating your heart by addressing those wounds and pushing into your deepest desires.

Ten

HOW TO ACTIVATE YOUR HEART

Life is alchemy, and emotions are
the fire that turns me to gold.

GLENNON DOYLE, *UNTAMED*

Bravo for having the courage to step outside of yourself to notice the woman you have become! As you walk through your past in order to put language to your life equity, you may come across painful experiences you'd rather overlook. I call these moments *wounds* because they are places where we have unresolved hurt or spaces where our heart has been made tender to the touch of the world.

No matter how good our lives have been, as we re-author our stories, it's only natural to discover a handful of moments that still feel sore. These aren't necessarily catalytic events. Nevertheless, we need to tend to them before we can rush on with our life purpose.

At their best, these spaces will soften you to be a positive force in the world. As I've shared, they can be a source of your life equity, giving you direction for where to apply your talents. That's the redemptive version. But I'd be remiss not to mention that at their worst, these wounds ooze and pus, causing chaos and distraction that keep you from living out your purpose. The hardships you've suffered or conflicts that have yet to be resolved will inevitably become barriers to your purpose because they interrupt the flow of genius. In the book of Hebrews, we're told to "throw off everything that hinders and the sin that so easily entangles."[1] Well, this is the stuff that hinders. Your wounds turn into obstacles if left unaddressed.

Think about it in a physical sense. Imagine you are walking around with a gaping flesh wound and no bandage. In that state, a simple trip to Target to grab some snacks could put you at risk of further injury. An unsuspecting lady trying to reach for Cheetos might bump into you in aisle 12, and then boom—you're in massive pain and screaming while she apologizes, confused by what just happened.

That's the same response we have to the psychological and emotional wounds that are still exposed. Open and vulnerable, we head out into the world—and then get triggered by passersby in seemingly innocuous situations. Then we spend the rest of the day fuming, weeping, or disintegrating as a result of harmless interactions.

BINDING YOUR WOUNDS

What I'm saying is: You have to bind your wounds. To bind them means to take time to proactively find healing in the places you've been harmed or hurt. This might mean getting into professional therapy, going on a personal reflective retreat, or intentionally taking time to reflect on and process the past. Choose the pathway that works best for you.

For now, take a quick glance back into your story and notice what has yet to be resolved. What past sticking points or thorns in your side can still cause distraction and reactivity in the present? Did you stumble upon any while walking through your life narrative? Grab them all. Because these are the spaces that will cause you to put your head underwater again and lose sight of who you are. Your wounds will drive you to interact with the world as the old self rather than the whole self you are meant to be.

If you're not sure if an experience has left a wound, a good way to decipher this is to look for conflict in your life. Where are you experiencing struggle? Ask yourself if there is any connection to something that happened in your past. I was trained as a family systems therapist, so I err on the side of thinking that says almost all of our challenges and responses were formed in those early years within our family of origin. In the therapy room, clients rarely react only to what's happening in the present, but rather to the holdover of deeper wounds that haven't healed. Is this true for you?

UNCOVERING YOUR CORE VALUES

Now here's the good news. Identifying wounds is worth your time—because when you know what they are, you can allow them to become places of sensitivity and wisdom rather than places for further injury. It's not all doom and gloom. When acknowledged and cared for, wounds shift into core values. In this redeemed state, these bound wounds become an asset, quickly reminding you how to live on purpose by redirecting you to what's most important. Your values become the guardrails of your version of the good life, setting the bounds of your purpose-affirming activity so you live in flow.

Values help us keep living courageously as women of consequence because they prompt us to protect what's vulnerable. They are quick, self-honoring reminders of our identity that allow us to silence external voices that cause us to lose our way. In speaking about the power of values, the always brilliant Brené Brown said, "If we do not have clarity of values, if we don't have anywhere else to look or focus . . . the cynics and the critics can bring us to our knees."[2]

I don't want you to end up back on your knees. We just did all this work to get you standing again in the power of your talents and slowly turning to face the direction God means for you to go. Let's not waste the effort. Be sure to take a moment to capture your values by going back into your story and binding the wounds you've suffered through the years. You've already identified your life equity, so you know the content of your heart space or the problem you are invested in solving. Noting these other wounds will guide you to the driving forces behind the specific content areas so you're always running in the right direction.

Let me give an example.

Personally, I have a lot of life equity in the space of women taking control of their lives to find their purpose. (I know . . . shocker.) If I told you my life story, you'd hear me talk a lot about studying the way people function and dreaming about how individuals impact the world. You'd also catch the pain in my voice when I talk about my mom. One of my strongest childhood memories is sitting on the floor of a bookstore when I was around eight years old. I loved to read, and my mom would take me to get a book as a special treat when I did well in school. One day while I was paging through a new book I wanted to buy, she asked, "Chanel, do you know what you want to be when you grow up?"

I laughed and rattled off, "I want to be a writer like Terry McMillan or maybe a news reporter." She smiled back, delighted with my choices. And then her eyes started to glaze over.

I could tell something was off, so I asked, "What's wrong, Mommy?"

With longing and regret sitting in her throat, she said, "You're so lucky. I never knew what I wanted to be. No one ever asked me."

My mom grew up as the oldest of eleven kids, and as an adult, she later gave birth to three kids of her own. (My brothers and I are all about a decade apart from one another.)* Her life was dedicated to raising babies, and she never got the chance to live for herself.

"I guess life just passed me by," she reflected. "I was always waiting for my turn to live, and it never came."

That moment left a major wound in my life. I've grieved the purpose my mother never got to live. But as that wound has healed, it has become a guide for my life's greatest work. I don't want any woman to have to wait for her turn to live. So I have dedicated myself to helping women talk about their lives and apply language to their experience so they can articulate what they want. It's my sacred point of intersection within the world's deep hunger.

Behind my life equity of women taking control of their lives,

---

* Let that sink in for a second. That means my mom spent over fifty years raising children under the age of ten. She's basically a saint.

I have some deep wounds I've had to heal that now serve as values driving my life. When these deeper values are not respected, I feel out of whack. They serve as early warning signs to me that I'm beginning to veer off the path of my purpose. Here's another example.

One value I hold is collaboration, and it's the direct result of a wound I've carried with me for many years. To me, life is most worthwhile when I'm working alongside someone else to bring a vision to life. It's the reason I was so enamored by my old church's motto to "join God in the renewal of all things." I love the idea of being a collaborator with God. This value for collaboration is born out of several wounds I had as the baby girl in my family. There were many times throughout my life when I was left to myself to create, play, and dream alone. I often felt neglected. And when my family went through big transitions, such as my parents' separation or my mom's remarriage, I was left to make sense of these difficult family situations on my own. I felt lost in the shuffle and stuck problem-solving by myself.

As a result, I'm incredibly sensitive to people feeling like they are left out or people who feel isolated trying to understand problems in the world on their own. I believe people are better together, facing life's difficulties and working to solve challenges with each other's help. That's why I take the posture of "I'm with you" when working with clients. I want them to know they aren't in the uncertainty of life alone. Do you see how my values guide so many of the decisions I make every single day? They put into perspective many of the choices I've made throughout my life or the pathways I've chosen *not* to pursue, despite the times when it sounded like a good idea to everyone else.

What do you value? There probably aren't very many things

you'd list. I like the way Brené Brown challenges people to narrow their values to two because I agree that we have only about two to three main values that form the basis of what's important to us. Everything else is usually an iteration of the deepest values we treasure.

Go back and bind your wounds. Investigate each to see what redemptive value might be lurking beneath the pain. This is one of the most self-honoring exercises you will do. I'm including a long list of values I've put together to spark some ideas for you as you seek some language to describe who you are:

Abundance	Accountability	Achievement
Adaptability	Advancement	Adventure
Affection	Altruism	Ambition
Appreciation	Authenticity	Authority
Autonomy	Balance	Beauty
Belonging	Boldness	Career
Caring	Challenge	Change
Charisma	Clarity	Collaboration
Commitment	Commonality	Communication
Community	Compassion	Competency
Connection	Contentment	Contribution
Cooperation	Courage	Creativity
Curiosity	Determination	Differentiation
Dignity	Discipline	Diversity
Effectiveness	Efficiency	Encouragement
Endurance	Enjoyment	Entertain
Entrepreneurship	Environment	Equality
Ethics	Excellence	Excitement
Facilitation	Fairness	Faith
Fame	Family	Financial stability
Finesse	Fitness	Forgiveness
Freedom	Friendship	Fun
Future	Generosity	Giving back
Goodness	Grace	Gratitude
Growth	Harmony	Health

Home
Humanity
Inclusion
Initiative
Intelligence
Involvement
Kindness
Learning
Love
Openness
Parenting
Peace
Personal fulfillment
Popularity
Professionalism
Quality
Relationship
Renewal
Respect
Risk-taking
Self-respect
Significance
Spirituality
Stewardship
Teamwork
Tradition
Trustworthiness
Wealth
Willingness

Honesty
Humility
Independence
Innovation
Intuition
Joy
Knowledge
Legacy
Loyalty
Optimism
Patience
Perseverance
Pleasure
Power
Prosperity
Reciprocity
Reliability
Reputation
Responsibility
Safety
Serenity
Simplicity
Stability
Strength
Thrift
Travel
Vision
Wellness
Wisdom

Hope
Humor
Influence
Integrity
Invention
Justice
Leadership
Leisure
Nature
Order
Patriotism
Personal development
Poise
Pride
Purpose
Recognition
Religion
Resourcefulness
Rest
Security
Service
Speed
Status
Success
Time
Trust
Vulnerability
Wholeness

FEEDING YOUR FANTASIES

Now for the fun part. You've put language to your life equity, and you've noticed what values have been stirred as you bound your wounds. Now you get to lean into your desires. This is your chance to dream and get excited. I want you to take a moment to feed your fantasies.

What does that mean? To feed your fantasies is to give yourself intentional time and space to indulge the desires sitting latent in your heart. It is pausing to think about what you think about when you daydream. (It's very meta, to be honest.) But in this space of imagination, we allow a part of ourselves to run free—to push beyond the status quo of what we've come to accept as our reality. Do you ever do that, or are you all business all the time? How often do you allow yourself to dream and envision new possibilities without editing yourself or shifting into planning mode?

As much as your past matters in activating your heart, it's crucial to allow your hopes for the future to give you some direction as well. When you let your heart play, little fissures open in your brain, permitting new ideas and possibilities to settle in and shape the plans you have for your life. In that space you can generate new solutions and creatively carry your talents into new territory.

I owe almost all of my success to the fantasies I permitted myself to have when I was young. While I know my talents and tapping into my life equity helps me, the fantasies I hold for my future have continued to inspire and pull me along. I am intent on making my dreams reality.

What about you? What kinds of dreams do you have for the world? Or let me ask that another way. If you could set the world right on its axis, what would you want to see change or develop? You get to be God for a moment. And just like when God created the earth by speaking everything into existence, imagine all you need to do is say the word and things will be put in their proper place. What does your perfect world look like? What gets you excited? I'm talking about the whole world, not just your life.

You don't have to figure out a plan for how to accomplish

anything right now. Your fantasies aren't SMART goals,† so don't cut them off at the ankles before they even get going. You don't need specificity, and metrics don't matter. Go ahead and let your mind run free. Spend time imagining what you'd like to see exist in the world, and write it down. Create a laundry list of ideas you can edit later. See what emerges. You might surprise yourself.

Women so frequently censor themselves. In life-planning sessions, I've trained myself to always take the extra beat. By that, I mean that when a woman is mentioning something she longs for, I try to pause and give her one more beat to verbalize the thought and get it out into the open. Because I watch women leave most of their best ideas on the table—life-changing stuff that would be radical in helping the world—because they have already shut themselves down or decided they are being "silly" or "self-indulgent" with their desires.

One woman I worked with had a fantasy of opening up a creative space for people in her local community to authentically connect. Another had an idea for a new liquor company using a rare kind of vegetable she dreamed of bringing to market. One woman wanted to write poetry that was research-based and genre-blending, and another had a dream of coming alongside the families of musicians so they could stay rooted together. Each wanted to diss and dismiss their own fantasies of what could be before the ideas even got off the ground. How many of your dreams have been stunted because you cut off their wings before they could attempt flight?

---

† You have permission to be impractical for a moment. Very few genius ideas started off specific, measurable, achievable, relevant, or time-bound. I mean, Suzy Batiz invented Poo-Pourri by dreaming of a world where she could get rid of bathroom smells with essential oils. Anything is possible. Let your mind run free.

Let's play for a minute, friend. Carve out some space to imagine the many different ways you might want to have impact in the world. Dream of what could be and explore the ways in which you might influence our society. Just be sure to dream out loud so these gems don't stay trapped in your head. Here are a few practical ways you can feed your fantasies:

- **JOURNAL.** You've already got that Reclaim the Morning time established. See? I was looking out for you all those chapters ago, encouraging you to create space for routinely finding your footing. Spend some time journaling about all the big ideas you have.
- **SHARE WITH PEOPLE.** Talk to anyone and everyone about the things that excite you. As you share your passions and the dream you have for the world you want to see, you practice articulating a vision that can guide you. Plus, you position yourself to encounter other people who may also want to see that vision come to light. We'll talk about position and influence in the next chapter, but I'll say now that quite often women have resources and support at their disposal they never leveraged simply because no one knew they could use the help.
- **RESEARCH.** Look for other people or organizations who are already working in the space you're envisioning to some degree. There is truly nothing new under the sun. If you've had a good idea, someone else probably had it too. However, the way they are approaching it may be different from how you'd engage the same issue. And they don't have the same combination of talents as you. Find out if there are ways for you to participate or help someone

who is already doing what you care about. You may find yourself collecting lifelong running mates in your purpose zone or discovering a great temporary space to kick-start your vision.

- **GET PROXIMAL.** Move closer to the issues you most care about to keep your heart tender and your motivation high. You can do this by seeking out relationships with people who are dealing with the problems you dream of solving or by finding ways to listen to their struggles from a distance. For example, one of my past clients had a heart for justice, and due to the pandemic that dominated 2020, she wasn't able to physically be around the men and women she wanted to serve. While she waited for COVID-19 restrictions to be lifted so she could go back to serving in person, she started watching documentaries and reading books about or by people who were experiencing the injustices she wanted to address. This helped her stay proximal to their suffering and continue to keep her heart tender as she fantasized about new ways to help them.

Through the seasons, as you continue to stoke the fires of your dreams, the direction for your life will evolve and become more nuanced. Let it grow over time. You don't have to make this your day job or focus all of your energy on solving a problem or trying to redeem the world. Remember, you are a colaborer with Christ. It's not all on your shoulders, so don't take the full weight of the world on yourself. It's okay to activate your heart to varying degrees and through different means throughout the seasons of your life. Remember that you are crafting a life mission, not a career or launching a business.

REVISITING YOUR LIFE
PURPOSE STATEMENT

Speaking of mission, let's look at your life purpose statement again. Remember that quick statement you wrote down in chapter 6? Dig it out from the bottom of that pile on your desk or flip back in your journal or phone notes to see what you wrote. Does it still hold up based on the new perspective you've gained over the past couple chapters? You've mentally covered a lot of ground. In light of that, how might you change or adapt your purpose statement?

Here are some questions for consideration based on what we've explored:

- Is your purpose statement large enough, specific enough, and flexible enough to last you through the whole of your life?
- Does your purpose statement nod to your specific talents and seem consistent with how God uniquely uses you in the world?
- Does your purpose statement connect to your heart space, taking into account the life equity you've built, honoring the values you carry, and fueling you to live into the fantasies you hold of a redeemed world?

Wordsmith your life purpose statement. It should be brief and targeted to motivate you as you begin to take action and live out your version of the good life. Take your time. There is so much to be experienced over time. As my Nigerian mother-in-law used to say, "Don't rush to eat a feast." Your purpose awaits you, so just take it in, bite by bite.

Friend, I wish we were sitting together so I could really check in on how you're doing. How is all of this feeling for you? Do you feel your shoulders broadening a bit? I sure hope so. You really are an incredible example of God's workmanship. I need you to know that. And I'm so grateful that someone just like you exists on this planet to make ripples in the river of culture in the way only you can. Thank you for being you. I mean it.

Isn't it funny that you started out drowning, trying to live someone else's life, when you were wired for this kind of greatness? You thought a promotion would make you worthy, a great night in bed would set your soul on fire, or a new pair of red-bottomed shoes would unlock your power. No way! The life you've been moving away from—that ordinary life you thought was inadequate—is exactly the life that will be most fulfilling for you.

Let's start to get a little momentum with a heave-ho out of the shallow water. I want to help you begin stewarding the influence you have to make a powerful contribution in the world. You up for it? I'll see you in the next chapter.

eleven

THE SHIFT FROM FEAR TO EXCITEMENT

Do not merely listen to the word, and so deceive
yourselves. Do what it says. Anyone who listens to
the word but does not do what it says is like someone
who looks at his face in a mirror and, after looking
at himself, goes away and immediately forgets
what he looks like. But whoever looks intently into
the perfect law that gives freedom, and continues
in it—not forgetting what they have heard, but
doing it—they will be blessed in what they do.

JAMES 1:22-25

I love big vision, don't you? It's so much fun to think in the abstract, pushing the limits of our imagination to re-author our lives or consider new possibilities. When we lack vision, we feel lost and distracted. We are easily wooed by lesser things. Just the thought of a large framing vision to guide our actions gives me life!

By now you've crafted a revised life purpose statement that is deeply rooted in the core of who you are and what you do (your identity), and your purpose is aimed at what you uniquely care about in the world (your direction). This is exciting stuff because it's possible you already have a new picture coming into focus for the life you're meant to live. That vision alone may be giving you all the feels, and you're thinking, *Well, this has been great, Chanel. I'm ready to pack up and move on with all the perspective I've gained.*

But slow down, Speed Racer. Perspective is important, which is why we've spent the bulk of our time trying to orient ourselves and learn more about who we are. But if you really want to do that heave-ho out of the shallow water, we need to nail down an action plan. You've got to *do something* with all the insight you've gleaned.

Up to this point you've collected many little facts about how you operate in the world. Some of this information has been brand-new. Some details you were already aware of, and some things you sensed but never put language to until now. But all of that information adds up to a whole lot of nothing if we don't pull it together. The "Ready, aim . . ." part of the process doesn't have much oomph if you never get to "fire!" I want to wrap up this self-discovery process with you by helping you distill all we've walked through into a handful of action steps you can take to begin living into your version of the good life—starting this week.

But I have to be honest first. Your eyes might start to glaze over as I push you to be specific. It's not you; it's me. No, wait a minute. I meant to flip that. It's not me; it's you. Your brain is about to slip into self-protection mode, and I want you to be aware of that because it's the reason why taking action can be so darned difficult. This is the moment when you will want to protect the insufficient life you've already been living. And because of that, you'll be tempted to tune me out or find something else to do.

Suddenly that pile of laundry feels urgent. Or you could use a nap. (I mean, you have been reading for a while.) Maybe you can scroll Facebook for a bit and see what happened to that old flame that crossed your mind while you were redeeming your history. This is your official warning that you're going to want to find something to distract you or disconnect you from letting go of the old life you were living and taking action toward the new life you've started to envision. It's all good; I won't take it personally. Your response is perfectly normal.

A NORMAL RESPONSE TO THE UNKNOWN

In this space of convergence, where big, abstract thinking intersects with concrete, practical steps, I find that clients often want to drag their feet. You might feel that way too. It's almost like a panic response where you freak out* in the face of danger. The new life you're being invited to live feels like a threat because it's unfamiliar territory, so you either flee (by running back to the life you lived before), fight (by attacking me and my "dumb, totally unhelpful process"), or freeze (by being paralyzed between the old life and the new).

In therapy we refer to this as an acute stress response, during which you experience diffuse physiological arousal. You've probably

---

* That's another highly technical term, by the way.

heard of this already as the "fight-or-flight response," a term that was originally coined by psychologist Walter Bradford Cannon. He concluded that animals experienced an adrenaline surge in response to emergencies, both physical (such as sudden trauma or blood loss) and psychological (such as—get this—having your old mental framework and idea of success ripped away from you).[1]

And while this response is meant to compel you to move toward safety, it can be incredibly problematic. For our purposes, when you're in this state, your mind starts to work against you. Here's why.

When someone is flooded by a stress response driven by fear, there are very real consequences. Here are just a handful of things you might experience:

- You can't take in or process new information.
- You begin to shut down emotionally.
- You get stuck in repetitive thought loops, circling around the same ideas again and again.
- You lose access to your sense of humor.
- You struggle with creative problem-solving.
- You lack empathy and can't see things accurately from someone else's perspective.
- Everything begins to feel urgent and integrated, with stress from one area pouring over into the other.

In short, feeling afraid or threatened by uncertainty can sabotage all the hard work you've already done and all the possibilities you have for your future. And unfortunately, it's the way that a perfectly reasonable person (yes, I'm still talking about you) might respond. In fact, it's the way most of my clients respond as we near the end of information gathering and start to pull the details together into a cohesive plan. Afraid you're about to get hurt, you might switch to self-protective mode. Panic is a natural response to perceived danger.

One client in particular sticks out in my mind as someone who panicked the moment we started moving into action. Let me tell you about Eunice.

Eunice: Hitting the Wall of Fear

Eunice was ecstatic throughout the self-discovery portion of our time together. She loved putting language to her talents and had big hopes of using them on her LinkedIn profile to attract future employers. She also felt validated after unpacking her heart space because she said the exercises illuminated the kinds of organizations she wanted to support financially with her tax return the following year. But as we got into the planning part of her session—the moment when she needed to actually commit to taking action with dates, times, and locations—I started to feel her resistance. She kept asking to take bathroom breaks, her jawline tightened, and her eyes glazed over as I spoke. I tried not to take it personally, but when someone yawns four times in your face, it's easy to start wondering if you're the reason.

I recalled my early training in family therapy when I was taught to read an infant's body language to discern how they are feeling. Eunice was giving me major "I'm overstimulated and need a nap" vibes. So I stopped pushing. I let her off the hook with a few tiny commitments that would at least get her moving, though not address the full scope of what she could do. We recapped all she'd learned, and I packed up her flip charts to send her home.

As soon as she left, I drank a glass of red wine and ate

cheesecake before falling asleep to *The Notebook*—because sometimes therapists can't cope either. I felt terrible about our work together for months. Was I a failure? I know the difference I can make in a client's life, and I was disappointed she didn't have a radical transformation. But I kept repeating my coaching mantra—"I'm responsible to my clients, not for them"—in order to keep a healthy boundary between the work and my self-worth.

Then a funny thing happened. Later that fall Eunice sent me a three-page email outlining the specific shifts she'd made. She praised me for my patience and admitted she just wasn't ready to let go of her old life when we met. She wrote,

> Thank you for not pushing me beyond the places I was ready to change. I was so terrified to let go of how I knew to operate in the world. I just couldn't imagine living any differently in that moment. I was scared trying a new way would leave me hurt. But I've spent some time grieving the life I lost to chasing success, and I gave myself permission to admit I hated how things used to be. I even started therapy—can you believe it? I'm okay not being okay, and I'm grateful you let me have the space to start putting my life together the way I want it to look. I'm excited to see the seeds that we planted grow during my life-planning retreat.

I guess we didn't fail after all.

So that's Eunice's story of hitting the wall of fear. But why might someone like you—someone who has felt safe throughout this whole process—suddenly start to feel like she's going to get hurt? You're not scared of me, right? I mean, I'm a nice person.[†]

---

† Plus, I'm five feet tall with the upper-body strength of a kindergartner, so you can take me.

Why would you resist going on this journey with me as we shift from abstract to concrete thinking and commit to an action plan? Let's talk about that for a second.

REASONS TO FEEL AFRAID

You might be afraid to commit to action right now for a whole host of reasons. But here are the internal questions my clients struggle to answer.

What if I fail?

You might be worried you're going to take in all this information you learned about yourself, start to put it into action, and completely tank. What if the business you start doesn't go anywhere, or what if you put yourself out there in a relationship and get nothing in return? What if you try and nothing comes of it? Let me kindly say that you'd be no worse off than you are now. It's trite, I know, but as the saying goes, "You miss 100 percent of the shots you never take." It's a fact! When you don't try, you've already lost. To combat this way of thinking, you have to reframe how you view failure. Failing miserably is not the same as making a mistake. Failure is a natural part of the research-and-development phase of life. As you work toward solutions, it's inevitable that you'll also discover options that don't work. Failure just narrows the path to success. I love to fail. I especially love to fail quickly. Because the sooner I fail at one thing, the sooner I can close the door and move on to another possibility that might succeed. I want to encourage you to reframe failure. Fail fast and thoroughly if you want to live your version of the good life.

What if I'm not as good as I think I am?

This question smacks of imposter syndrome. And to be honest, you don't have time for it. There is too much at stake because we need you to do the thing you are meant to do in the world. We don't have time to worry about your being good enough. As my friend Regan Walsh wrote in her book, *Heart Boss*, "You've got to be brave before you can be good."[2] Everyone starts out as an imposter. Before we begin, we have no proof we are who we believe ourselves to be. Let yourself be a beginner. And in the doing, you'll prove you are who you say you are. Risk being an imposter. When I first started writing for magazines, I felt so insecure pitching myself. I was fresh out of college, and I thought, *Who am I that these big editors would take me seriously?* My mentor Michelle Burford, who has written books for everyone from Alicia Keys to Cicely Tyson, gave me this advice. She said, "Chanel, if you write about anything three times, you're an expert." I know now she wasn't speaking literally. She was trying to shake me out of my inertia by encouraging me to make at least three attempts. She's an abundance-mindset ninja.‡ I want to tell you the same. You are who you say you are. You're only an imposter when you start. Everyone is, so that's okay. Give yourself the chance to make three big efforts at doing whatever it is you're most afraid of, and then stop calling yourself an imposter. After three times, you can decide if you're an expert or if you need to abandon the effort.

What if other people judge me?

Who are these people? Give me their names and Instagram handles, because I would like to have a word with them. Look, I

---

‡ I owe so much of who I am to Michelle Burford, a woman who has modeled excellence in the pursuit of purpose for nearly twenty years for me.

don't want to be insensitive to your mini bout of social anxiety, but you're not in high school. No one is thinking about you. They really aren't. About 103 percent of the time, people are operating out of their own wounds, hopes, and needs. Plus, you are a grown woman. I'm not going to let you sit back and miss your whole life purpose because you're worried about what the girls wearing pink over at the other lunch table might think of you. If people judge you, they judge you. Expect it. In fact, a lot of people are not going to like you. They will be angry and jealous that you got out of the rat race of chasing significance. Let them be bitter. Their self-discovery journey is not yours. Usually when people express doubt, I find it's a statement about their own capacity—not mine. Maybe it's hard or impossible for them, but not for you. Don't be held back by the ceiling on someone else's life.

What if I don't choose the "right" thing?

Well this is an easy one, because there is no one right thing. Life is not the summation of one decision. It's a series of tiny choices we make day after day. If one decision leads you somewhere you don't want to go, make another choice. God's mercies are new every morning.[3] In high school, I was a theater kid, which should come as no surprise to you by this point. Don't I have "I wanted to be the lead in the spring play" written all over me? One of my favorite things we did to warm up was to play improvisation games at the start of class. The best game was New Choice. The rules are simple. You're put in a situation and told to start acting out a scene. For example, someone would say, "You're in an ice cream shop picking out your favorite flavor." Then the audience periodically yells out "New choice," and you have to think on your feet and choose something else. "I'd love to have a vanilla cone." *New choice!* "Actually, I think I'd like strawberry with sprinkles." *New choice!* "I'd like a banana split with a hot dog on top." You get the idea. It would go on and on, getting more absurd by the minute. I loved it. I loved how it taught me to detach from my decisions and think outside the box, because there is always a new choice to be made. Even when life seems really good, something unexpected is always lurking around the corner as an option— and it might just be the perfect ending to your scene.

What if I'm fundamentally broken?

Are you hesitating to make a plan because you suspect that if things go off the rails, the problem is you? Maybe you fear you're messed up, and you don't want to go any further because you're trying to protect yourself from confirmation that you're broken. But this is a lie. You are not broken. Go back to the start of chapter 7 and reread the list of what's true about who you are. If all the things God says about you are true, what meaning could you make about your lack of success? You might choose an alternative interpretation. Instead of "I'm broken," you might choose to believe "God has something more in store for me that is yet to be revealed." If you set aside the "I'm a mess" lie, maybe you could think it's possible that something in your old life simply needs to be resolved before you can step into the new. There could be a whole host of reasons you don't immediately nail it; your being broken or flawed is not the only possible explanation. Be patient with yourself. Choose the most favorable interpretation, and keep moving.

These are all very real fears to have, and I hope by naming them you're able to push past the limiting beliefs embedded in those questions that cause you to stay stuck.

Regardless of what's tripping you up and keeping you from committing to an action plan, I want to introduce a mindset shift that will empower you to get real momentum around stepping into your version of the good life. In order to move out of a fight-or-flight response, you have to flip from fear to excitement.

FLIPPING OUT OF FEAR

Excitement and fear are really two sides of the same coin. They are both responses to the unknown. But excitement is a courageous response. It's the kind of posture a woman of consequence takes when she has decided to live from the inside out and stopped doubting herself. Excitement says, *I don't know what's coming, but I believe I have what it takes to navigate whatever comes my way.* Excitement also says, *I am looking forward to an opportunity to see myself in action against the reality of the world.* It's a positive anticipation of the future.

Fear, on the other hand, is a dread response. Fear says you will not be able to live up to the moment, and you will be overtaken by what's coming. Fear makes you worry because fear is negative anticipation in the face of uncertainty. I read somewhere that the Bible tells us "do not fear" about 365 times, one reminder for every day of the year, because God's clever like that. God knows we're wired to panic the second we enter new experiences or get activated in our purpose. So he reminds us to reject fear again and again and again. We need to choose excitement.

Did you know you could do that? Emotions can be chosen. You don't have to be the victim of your automatic responses. Because if God says "do not fear" that many times, it must mean you have the power to opt out of the fear response and turn toward your future with positive anticipation. You can expect victory. Never forget you are entitled to the good life—*your* good life, rooted in your talents and heart. That is the victory we are seeking.

We need to get you into an excited state so you can remain creative and start seeing solutions that weren't there when you first started this process. Because when you're excited, you flip all of those stress responses I mentioned earlier on their head.

- Instead of fearing new information, you actively scan your environment looking for new insight.
- Instead of emotionally shutting down, you keep yourself open to new possibilities.
- Instead of ruminating, you quickly evaluate and eliminate options.
- You experience giddiness instead of losing access to your sense of humor.
- You become creative and solutions-focused instead of struggling to solve problems.
- You recapture your empathy as you see connections between yourself and others.
- You move intentionally instead of urgently, focused on where you're headed and compartmentalizing challenges so you can tackle one issue at a time.

Doesn't that sound like a more helpful way to take action in your life? Forget fear; it doesn't serve you. Let's get excited!

And you know what gets me excited? Leaning into the idea of stewardship. Remember how I said your life purpose lies at the intersection of your talents, your heart, and your influence? Let's talk about what it means to steward your influence.

twelve

HOW TO STEWARD YOUR INFLUENCE

Do the work and show up for your life,
because you are the only one who can
live it, and the rest of us need you.

JEN HATMAKER, *FIERCE, FREE, AND FULL OF FIRE*

When it comes to owning your influence in the world, I use the language of stewardship intentionally. *Merriam-Webster* defines *stewardship* as "the conducting, supervising, or managing of something; especially: the careful and responsible management of something *entrusted to one's care*" (emphasis mine).[1] Therefore, when we steward our influence, we recognize that our lives are not our own to manage. We accept that the talents we have at our disposal and the passions we hold in our hearts are all means of influence we've been given by God to use toward a redemptive end.

You don't have to live a grandiose life that makes headlines. That might happen incidentally, but worldly significance is not the goal. Your responsibility is to faithfully oversee what you already have—your talents, heart, family, network, possessions, health, community, and more—so that what has been *entrusted to your care* might flourish on your watch.

This gets me excited, and I hope it gets you excited too. Because it makes taking action and starting to step into our version of the good life a more focused effort. When we lean into ways to steward our influence, we stay centered on joyfully examining what we have rather than obsessing over what we lack. And we keep asking questions like, "What is the next right thing to do?" rather than sinking under the weight of a lifetime of decisions. I'm much less afraid of thoughtfully considering what to do with the life I'm living right now than I am about trying to make some big splash in the world. I hope you are as well.

This idea of stewardship has been critical for so many of my clients when it comes to galvanizing them into action toward their life purpose. One client shared, "I was anxious about coming out of our life-planning intensive because I thought I would have to develop a massive business idea or have a grand plan to show for the investment. I was terrified everything would have to change in my life. But that's not where we landed at all. Sure, I might start a business one day, but I have more important plans. I know exactly what matters to me, and I have a new vision for what it looks like for each part of my life to thrive. So all I have to do is take responsibility for slowly inching everything in my life forward bit by bit. It's so liberating."

When we focus on stewardship, we don't need to have everything figured out #rightthisverysecond. We simply manage what we have now to the best of our ability, and then once that's gone as far as it can go, we see if there is anything else within our sphere of influence that we can help flourish next.

So let's get going. You can't sit in this kiddie pool forever. We have to get you out there living your best life. Let's get you stewarding your influence by assessing where you are, outlining your limits, and creating a realistic action plan.

ASSESS YOUR PRESENT

To get you moving, let's do another quick life assessment. This one is a little different from the one we did back in chapter 4 as we looked for signs of your life liturgies. Rather than considering how you're doing in general, this is more like taking inventory. We need to take stock of where you are right now and pay attention to the resources and pathways already before you. Terence Lester, an activist and the founder of Love Beyond Walls, said, "A huge part of growth is connected to humility. You have to humble yourself where you currently are in order to become the next best version of yourself."[2] Once you know where you are, you can get strategic about how to get where you want to go.

This pause in the process is a lot like going to the mall and taking a moment to review the store directory. You know you want to grab a new shirt at Madewell and maybe find a pair of shoes at Nordstrom. But before you can plan the most efficient route to get where you want to go, you have to find that big You Are Here label on the map. Also, take note of where the restrooms are. Until you locate yourself, you can't decide how to get where you want to go.*

We've already done some of this process for you by identifying

---

* For the record, it inevitably takes me about three minutes just to find the You Are Here label. So I apologize to everyone who has had to look over the shoulder of the girl standing there like an idiot taking forever. But locating yourself can be hard, okay!

who you are and what you're capable of doing in the world. We have your partial location. But we haven't cataloged all of the resources at your disposal or taken note of where God has placed you right now.

Let's slow down and look at where you're currently positioned. You know the drill by now. I'm going to ask you to write your answers down, so go ahead and grab that notebook you've been using. Here are some questions to consider.

Who do you know?

Lots of times when we want to start living out our purpose, we forget about the people right under our noses who can support us as we go. Take a moment to audit your group of friends and family members. Are you already in a relationship with people who may share your heart's passion or who may be happy to invest in anything you do in your heart space? What kind of people have you connected with through the years? Think about past colleagues and current social media connections. Consider all the acquaintances circling your life in your neighborhood and community who might be assets to you. Is there anyone from your past with whom you've lost touch, someone who might be the perfect connection to get you going in the direction you're headed? Take a minute to review the people you know. (Pro tip: I like to scroll through all the people who are following me on social media and then all the folks I'm following to see if anyone sparks ideas.)

Which networks or organizations are you a part of?

Where are you already connected? Think about the church you attend, the charities you support, the community clubs and Facebook groups you've joined. Jot down your high school or college alma mater, and definitely note a sorority if you were a part of one during school. Write all of them down because these are resources you can tap into later. You might have a much richer social circle than you imagine. This is also a good time to note any causes you have supported in the past or that you're currently supporting that might align with your talents or your heart.

Where are you located?

I'm speaking geographically. Do you live in the suburbs, country, or city? Are there any cultural changes or societal shifts unique to where you live or work that might be noteworthy for you? For example, when my family moved into the rapidly changing neighborhood of Bedford-Stuyvesant in Brooklyn, we were selective about the businesses we supported. City gentrification is complicated, so we chose to continue investing in older businesses that pre-existed us, while also supporting some of the new restaurants giving back to the neighborhood. Now that we have a home in the 'burbs outside Atlanta, I think a lot about the intersection of race, faith, and politics in an atmosphere that is charged with social change. What kind of landscape are you living in now, and what implications might place have on your purpose?

What kind of time or margin do you have?

I know you're busy, because it's after the year 2000 and you have a Wi-Fi connection. Everyone is busy. None of us has time for anything. But if you allowed yourself to move past that thought, what kind of time or margin do you *actually* have? Few of us are as busy as we think. My clients often have long stretches of time hiding in plain sight that they lose to escapism, overworking, or people-pleasing. What about you? Mentally walk through a typical week in your life and assess where your time goes. Do you have any usable moments? Is it a couple of free hours every third Saturday? Do you have an upcoming month when your schedule is about to lighten up for the season? If you stopped binge-watching *Friends* on HBO Max, cut down on social media, or hired someone to help you with household chores every other week, what kind of additional time or margin might you have available to use on purpose-driven projects? Whatever you see, write it down so we can track it. You'll want to be realistic with what kind of time you have at your disposal so you can intentionally use it later.

What financial resources do you have?

Think about your money situation. You don't need to be a millionaire to begin funding your own passions. Even a small amount of money can be invested or used as a kick-start for a portfolio that can later be leveraged for your purpose. Think about anything you own that you could liquidate or sell for financial resources if needed. You don't have to make any moves right now. We're just observing. Count up what you have.

Do you own or have access to anything unique?

Is there any place, item, or service you have special access to that could be used toward your purpose? For example, I own a home in Georgia, but I also have access to an office space in New York City where my husband and I run a therapy practice. Both locations can be used as safe spaces to see women as I help them develop their life purpose. I'm on the board of a nonprofit for start-ups doing good called Plywood People, and they have a coworking space. Maybe I could one day use it for something. I also have access to some church buildings in communities where I used to serve, and a family friend has a vacation home in the

Dominican Republic they might let me use. I'm not sure how it could be valuable in this particular moment beyond me getting some sun, but I'd write it down anyway. One day it might be just the place I need to implement the next phase of my purpose.[†]

Once you have all this information down on paper, you don't have to do anything with it. You've just created a massive inventory of everything you have at your disposal. We often feel out of control because we're not being resourceful enough with our lives. We think we have few options and nothing at our fingertips to move forward, so we stay stuck. This list will debunk that lie for you. I trust that you have more resources available to you in your life than you've imagined.

Continue to build on this list and review it through the years. These resources, combined with all that you've learned about who you are and what you do, will be beneficial to you at some point. Like the Bluth family used to say on the cult classic TV show *Arrested Development*, "There's always money in the banana stand."[3] This is your banana stand. You will never lack for resources if you leverage this list. There is gold in your inventory!

LOVE YOUR LIMITS

Now that you've assessed all you have, I want you to specifically take note of one untapped resource most people ignore. In fact,

---

† Did someone say, "Start taking clients on luxury life-planning retreats in DR"? Yes, please!

it's a resource so often overlooked that it can be mistaken for an impediment to purpose rather than an asset if you're not careful. I want you to consider for a moment the limits you have in your life. Are there fixed obstacles you sense are restraining you from the life you want to live? I know it's counterintuitive, but these limits may actually be tremendous resources you have not leveraged.

When I say limits, I'm not talking about limiting beliefs. Those kinds of limits don't serve us well. In fact, I'm going to give you five tools to combat some common limiting beliefs in the conclusion to this book. Right now I'm talking about literal limits (such as lack of time, energy, social capital, or money) that you suspect are holding you back from pursuing the good life.

For example, some of my clients will say things like, "Chanel, I'd like to pursue my purpose, but I can't because I'm a mom. I'm too preoccupied with raising babies to live out my calling." Others might say, "I just don't have enough time in the day to go after my purpose. I'll start taking action later in life when I have more margin or more help." These are the kinds of limits I want to invite you to start reconceptualizing as opportunities, because I believe your life expands in your limits. Hear me out on this.

One of my favorite modern thinkers is Kate Harris. She's the author of a Barna Frames book called *Wonder Women: Navigating the Challenges of Motherhood, Career, and Identity*. Harris is also a phenomenal speaker on calling and constraint. I had the privilege of meeting her years ago when we shared a meal in downtown Manhattan just before she spoke at an event I was hosting in Tribeca. I loved her immediately. She's the kind of woman you want to be best friends with because she manages to discuss raising kids, reading Ta-Nehisi Coates, and eating

Mexican food with the ease and fluidity of Savannah Guthrie on the *TODAY Show*.

I love how Harris wrote in her book about taking the Uniform Project challenge. The challenge was an idea that was originated in 2009 by a woman named Sheena Matheiken, who pledged to wear the same little black dress for the entire year. As much as Matheiken was making a statement on sustainability in fashion, she also sparked commentary on the power of restraint in creativity. She ultimately used the pledge as a fundraiser to provide uniforms for children in India and ended up raising over $100,000. Since then, many women have created their own iteration of this challenge, editing their wardrobe down to a uniform and watching the creativity flow.

So why am I telling you about this little black dress challenge? Well, for one, I'm named after Coco Chanel, and thereby obligated to make a fashion reference at least once in every piece I write. I wedged that one in there at the eleventh hour, so I'm feeling pretty good right now. I also wanted to introduce you to the Uniform Project because of how it shaped Kate Harris's perception of limits and thereby influenced my own thinking about calling.

In *Wonder Women*, Harris wrote, "This little black dress showed me how constraints can, in fact, be the source of tremendous freedom, clarity, and creativity. It offered me a new construct for making sense of my constraints." Now listen to the insight she gained from wearing the same outfits every day: "I realized the project was able to achieve something creative, meaningful, and fun only because it was always the same dress as the foundation for each outfit. In fact, it was the very constraint of a daily routine that made the whole project so unexpected and imaginative."[4] In other words, limits forced innovation. It's precisely because she didn't have a ton of options that she had to stretch her personal framework for how she might dress.

Harris went on to write,

> Honoring limitation has a curious way of yielding abundance. It's easy to look at my own limitations in terms of time, energy, abilities, and finances, among others and see them as impediments to my calling. But the Uniform Project beckoned me to reconsider . . . to see my constraints not as problems to be solved but as the *means* for creativity and focus in my life and work.[5]

I'd like to beckon you to reconsider your limits as well. What if the constraints you see as obstacles are actually conduits of creativity, allowing you to expand and implement your purpose in ways you might not if they weren't in place?

There are so many ways to live your life. We're the generation of opportunity overload. We live in a time when it's not more options we need, but rather limits to rein us in and direct our steps. That's why I love my limits, and I hope you'll learn to love yours too. Your life's constraints will force you to get scrappy and prioritize what matters most. They will also help you move quickly rather than sink into the paralysis of analysis that occurs when you sit on the sidelines of life evaluating all the possible futures you could live. With fewer options, you'll make decisions faster and with more ingenuity. The doors that have been closed to you, the lack of resources that keep you from entertaining grander opportunities, the minimal time and access you have—these are all gifts that reduce the number of paths you could walk along to pursue your purpose. Embrace them.

What does this look like in reality? I'll share from my own life what it means to love my limits.

For the past five years I've been limited by parenthood, organizing my life largely around nap schedules, potty breaks, meal prep, and more. But this limitation of motherhood has been an incredible asset, informing much of how I work with women. I know firsthand what it's like to have very little time. I also know what it's like to feel powerless and unseen, as if I'm an extra or supporting actor in my own life. When I stopped bucking against the limit of motherhood and started asking what it could teach me, a new world opened up. Embracing my limits within motherhood has given me empathy for women who serve as caregivers in a way I wouldn't have otherwise. That's a tangible benefit that directly affects my business's bottom line. Clients hire me because they know I get it. They also know I give real solutions that work in the context of demanding lives.

Another way the limit of motherhood has served me is by shaping the services I offer. I am trained as a therapist, but you can imagine that most people want to see their therapist every week outside of normal business hours. Guess what? That's exactly when *my family* needs me to be available. So I had to ask myself, *If I believe God wants me to bring insight to women so they can break out of broken patterns, how can I do that most efficiently with the little time I have?* When I leaned into the limit, I decided to accept that I do not have the bandwidth to work with clients for years at a time, slowly getting them clarity in primetime evening hours. So I only work with women in VIP intensives. I spend two days getting my clients massive clarity and then send them on their way to manage their own lives with a clear life blueprint. It turns out that this format is valuable to women like me who want immediate breakthrough rather than slow evolution. What could be perceived as inadequacy of time (for example, my inability to coach people for years) turns out to be a limit that yields abundance, serving more clients in a unique and deeply transformative way.

What benefits could your life limits be presenting you now?

Take some time to identify the areas where you feel like you're limited. Then flip your perspective by saying to yourself, *This limit is good because . . .* Here's the trick: Force yourself to find an answer. That's a little bit of psychological jujitsu I'm teaching you on the sly. I used to use this trick in therapy all the time to help my clients deal with anxiety. When you force a positive interpretation, it helps you accept the present and your mind does backflips finding a solution that supports the positive belief. Oprah Winfrey once said, "All stress is caused by wanting this moment to be something it's not."[6] It's so true. If you want to break out of fear and stress, learn to love your limits through radical acceptance.

Speaking of anxiety, mental health expert and author Dr. Reid Wilson challenges us to take it a step beyond acceptance to embracing. He wrote the best book I've ever read on managing anxiety, called *Stopping the Noise in Your Head: The New Way to Overcome Anxiety and Worry.* He wrote, "Anxiety thrives on your resistance to uncertainty and to discomfort . . . You have to find a way to honestly, purposely, and willingly *welcome* your uncertainty and distress."[7] In other words, the more we resist anxiety, and in our case the anxiety associated with our limits, the greater power it has to overtake us. Our mind becomes preoccupied with trying to reject reality. This is a waste of time. Your limits are real. Don't resist what's staring you in the face. Love your limits.

Okay, you've got all your resources locked and loaded. We need to start listing the handful of things you can do next to apply your talents in your heart space. Leveraging your limits will open up opportunities and direction for small next steps you might otherwise have overlooked. Let's make an action plan.

START TAKING ACTION

You've made it! This is the final step in our process of moving you into your version of the good life. It's funny because this is where most people start, right? They ask what they should do with their life, then throw a bunch of stuff against the wall. I hope you see now that you didn't have enough information at the outset to figure out how to move forward in your life. But you put in the work, and now you have perspective. So let's do this.

When we talk about taking action on your purpose, we want to focus on long-term rhythms and strategies to keep you walking according to what God created you to do. But we also want to highlight immediate next action steps that will move you closer to living a fulfilling life. Let's start there by deciding what's most critical now to your thriving.

Go back through your notes and do a quick review of what you learned as you walked through the various exercises. Take a moment to recenter yourself, and then ask, *What would it look like to take one tiny step closer to implementing my talents or caring for my heart space in each bucket of my life?* Think small. Your goal is to come up with microchanges, not an ambitious lifelong game plan.

One of my dear friends, Danika Brysha, is a self-care expert and the founder of Self-Care Society. She often talks about taking tiny fail-proof action versus making major changes when developing new wellness habits. There is so much power in starting small because you set yourself up to experience immediate success that you can build on over time. Instead of creating a grand plan for change, consider what kind of small tweaks you might make for each bucket. For example, if I wanted to become more fit, I wouldn't commit to taking yoga classes five days a week starting next week. I'd commit to doing one or two yoga poses each morning when I wake up starting tomorrow. It's so doable, I'd have to . . . well, do it!

Swift, small movements are at the core of what it means to stop drowning in shallow water. Back when I was six years old with my head in the kiddie pool at Wild Rivers, I thought I was dying. I thought I needed a lifeguard or a massive boat to rescue me from my ultimate demise. As it turns out, all I needed was to lift my head about ten inches to completely save myself. The effort was minuscule, but it shifted my entire future.

The same is true for you when it comes to stepping into your version of the good life. You've been drowning in the search for significance, living someone else's version of thriving. Things have felt wildly out of whack, and you know you can't go on living this way one more day. But your rescue won't come from a major life overhaul. You don't need Iyanla Vanzant to fix your life. Instead, you need to make a handful of microchanges that can shift your life just a tad to get your head above water. From there, you'll make a few more changes, and then a few more, until you're swimming in the life of consequence that you want.

I've worked with enough women to know that you might have some resistance to making small changes and accepting that you'll have to keep adding steps as you go. Maybe you were reading this book, hoping to have a master plan by the end with turn-by-turn directions you can follow for the rest of your life. But it doesn't work that way. I mean, that's literally too much information for anyone to take in at one time. Plus, we want to leave room for you to be flexible and responsive to the new desires that will arise as you get to know yourself better through the years and the new opportunities that will come your way. Let's not trap you in another box, okay?

Start taking action on what's before you now. That's the fastest way to gain momentum around your purpose. Life rewards action. We take one step, and then four doors open up for us. I have no idea what your next commitments might be; everyone starts in a different spot. But here are some of the next steps my clients have taken immediately upon coming out of sessions with me that unlocked their whole lives:

- One woman decided to start having her morning yogurt and granola on her rooftop. It was that simple. Changing her breakfast location was her way of breaking through a lifetime pattern of workaholism and not allowing herself to pay attention to her personal needs. Instead of rolling out of bed and handing her life over to her job, she chose personal health by enjoying the New York City skyline before heading to the office. That choice allowed her to start making even more healthy decisions for her career and family life.
- Another client—an author—went through this process and committed to looking at prospective venues for a local community space she hoped to build. With little kids at home, she knew she was months away from starting the

project. But she wanted to stay inspired by physically walking into different buildings and dreaming of what kind of space she might eventually rent.

- A powerhouse entrepreneur spent a couple days with me reclaiming her vision for her career after a major professional setback. Her next action was to start cultivating friendships with heterosexual men. Outside of work, she knew she eventually wanted to get married and have kids, but most of her time was devoted to mobilizing other females. She was so unused to spending time with men that she needed to open herself up to new male relationships.

- An attorney I worked with decided to start reading books about different forms of spirituality. Her parents came from different faith backgrounds, and she had never managed to internalize either of their belief systems as her own. She loved her career and had a healthy partnership with the man of her dreams, but the question of who God was still gave her pause. She was eager to discover her own spirituality, so she set out as a beginner reading one book a month on different world religions.

- A publicist I coached decided to integrate her passion for personal development into her PR firm's ethos. As the business owner, she committed to facilitating growth opportunities for her staff through a voluntary monthly training or self-care opportunities that would reflect her value for wholeness and responsible living.

These were tiny changes based on where these clients started. But making these mini moves propelled them into the life they hoped to live.

What will it look like for you? Go through each life bucket, and based on what you've learned about yourself, dream of what it would mean for you to thrive in that space. Then decide the smallest action you could take in the direction of that vision of flourishing. There is no right answer. What feels right to you? Start with self and imagine what kind of woman you'd be if you were fully living out your purpose. Rested? Physically fit? Good at maintaining boundaries? What is one thing? Then choose an action you'd take in that direction. Once you have an action, move on to the other buckets. What tiny action could you take in your relationships? What career shift do you need to make? How can you deepen your spirituality? What global contribution can you make? Write everything down, commit to a plan, and build some accountability around it. Tell a friend, shout it from the rooftops, or declare it on social media. Just go all in on those small actions. Once you're done, ask yourself, *What can I do next?*

YOU'VE GOT THIS

You've got the blueprint, friend, to a life of consequence. Can you see it? Are you starting to imagine a new kind of life for yourself—something different from the one you've been living? Take a moment to visualize the woman you are becoming in full color. Picture your future self using the talents you've unlocked, moving into spaces that stoke your heart, and taking continual action to get results. Let your imagination come alive to your authentic life so you more instinctually move into liturgies rooted in the life vision you now hold.

I'm proud of the work you've done, and I can't wait to hear

about how your life evolves as you release that old way of living from the outside in and reclaim your voice. All you have to do is do it. Don't be a hearer and not a doer of your own word. Show up for yourself the way you'd show up for your best friend by following through on the steps you've chosen to take in line with the life you want.

Conclusion

SWIMMING LESSONS

We are what we repeatedly do. Excellence,
then, is not an act but a habit.

WILL DURANT, *THE STORY OF PHILOSOPHY*

We've reached the end, friend. I can't wait to see the good life you're going to live now—the one ordinary, extraordinary life that is completely unique to you.

When we started our journey together, I shared with you the power of liturgies to form your imagination and therefore shape your life. I want to end with a set of liturgies I hope will sustain you as you live the good life, rooted in your purpose. You've already assembled specific next action steps unique to your circumstances. Bravo! Commit to checking off those quick tasks and to-dos to get you moving in the right direction toward your purpose.

My hope is for you to embrace this set of lifelong postures that will intentionally reconnect you to your core identity no matter what life throws your way. It's not enough to keep you from drowning; I want to teach you how to swim. I want you to move with ease against the current of culture, holding on to who you are, even as you are subjected to competing ideals, beliefs, and visions of the good life that will woo you away from your unique purpose.

You know I'm always trying to prepare you for what's ahead—that's what a good guide does. I don't have all of life's answers, but I can tell you what you'll find around the bend. I've walked this path before you. And I've taken so many women through the process of finding their purpose that I can tell you with my eyes shut where you'll stumble and trip along your own road to meaning.

Real talk: There are bumps ahead, and the odds are against you. If you don't mind me mixing metaphors, I'll put it another way. You should anticipate some opposition because it's hard to move upstream, against the current of a culture that flows in the direction of significance. You're going to get flipped around, turned upside down, and thrown off course time and time again. That's the way real life works. It's unpredictable. Good things will happen that get you distracted. Like, Adele or Justin Timberlake will release a new album, and you'll lose hours streaming songs on Spotify—or maybe that's just me. Hardships will occur that leave you feeling powerless. People you love will make decisions that negatively affect you. Jobs won't pan out. Your landlord will sell your apartment building, and you'll move back in with your parents. Shoot, a pandemic will hit, causing the world to grind to a halt.

And with all that disruption, you might wonder if the truths you learned about yourself mean anything at all. In that space of self-doubt, you'll be enticed by the three lies of significance that pulled you underwater at the outset:

I am what I do.
I am who I love.
I am what I have.

We need to build in some life rhythms to remind you for the long haul that you, my darling, are so much more. So consider these your swimming lessons, like learning to do the butterfly stroke. I want to introduce you to the five postures of identity formation: silence, rest, generosity, gratitude, and play.

THE FIVE POSTURES OF IDENTITY FORMATION

I call them postures because they are simple to lean into, like moving into child's pose during yoga. These are meant to be gestures toward the kind of woman you are becoming. Each posture helps debunk those limiting beliefs that sabotage women on their road to purpose. Feel free to conform them into the shape that is most beneficial to you, as each posture is meant to adjust to your personal rhythm and style.

The only thing I ask is that you implement them as soon as possible. You have a wonderful future ahead of you, and I don't want your head to slip underwater again due to common lies that so easily take hold. If you lean into these purpose-affirming postures repeatedly, they will help you recenter whenever you're tempted to drift back into chasing a life of significance. Let's dive into them so I can help you climb out of those thought sinkholes you're likely to slip into as you move into the good life.

Silence

The first posture is an easy one, so let's begin with silence. You can give yourself a gold star because—surprise—you're already doing this! I told you I'm like a stealth mind ninja—I'm always working three steps ahead of you for your good. I set you up with the Reclaim the Morning practice all those chapters ago specifically to build silence into your life because I knew it would be critical to your long-term thriving. You need quiet. Especially at the start of your journey, when you're building up your self-confidence muscle, it's important to mute the opinions of others so you're not constantly looking to them to affirm that you're living your life in the "right" direction.

Approval- and validation-seeking are major risks at this point in your journey. You see, you've learned a lot about yourself, identifying your talents and even getting a big life purpose statement down on paper. If you feel excited about that, you'll likely want to shout it from the rooftops and start getting feedback from others. I encourage you to do so. Tell someone what you've discovered. Accountability is helpful in the pursuit of your purpose. Just don't let your support squad turn into a board of directors for your life. Affirmation can morph into approval real quick if you're not careful. So remember: If you don't need their permission, you don't need their approval.

And it's not just about beating the people-pleasing habit. Developing a posture of periodic silence in your life will help quiet the external narratives daily influencing you to become something you're not. The world is so noisy, and people scream at you all day with competing visions of the good life. Protect your ability to hear your own voice and to listen for the voice of God so you can stay in touch with your calling. Reclaiming the morning can be your safe space to check in with yourself.

I also encourage you to integrate silence into your life in other ways. You don't have to live like a monk to make this happen. Small habits, such as routinely checking out of social media or going on quarterly spiritual direction retreats, can be useful. Earlier I mentioned my friend Danika Brysha, who is a self-care expert. It's worth mentioning that she's also a social media influencer and professional model. Her life can be loud and chaotic. But she has developed a habit of silence by taking Mondays off social media, when she turns over her Instagram platform to other experts and lets them pour into her audience while she has a day for white space. It's a beautiful way to unplug and create silence.

One more thought. You know who else unplugged regularly? Jesus. Are you better than Jesus? I didn't think so.* Pastor John Mark Comer has a whole section of his book *The Ruthless Elimination of Hurry* devoted to how Jesus practiced silence and solitude. He notes how right after Jesus' baptism, the first thing he did was to go into the wilderness. He stepped into his calling (like you just did) and then immediately went to a quiet place. We often think of this moment negatively because the wilderness is where Jesus had a face-off with Satan. We think of Jesus as being vulnerable while alone and quiet. But Comer wrote that for Jesus, "The wilderness isn't the place of weakness; it's the place of *strength*."[1] In silence he was centered and able to hear the Father and himself. "From that place of emotional equilibrium and spiritual succor," Comer points out, "he knew precisely what to say yes to and, just as importantly, what to say no to."[2] Commit right now to lean into silence—regularly.

---

* We call this a "Jesus-juke" in my family. It's when someone takes the conversation in a spiritual direction so you can't argue with it. Gotcha!

Rest

The next posture you'll want to integrate into your life is rest. I'm talking deep soul rest where you intentionally suspend all productivity and simply exist. It might look like staring out the window at people passing by on the street, taking a midafternoon nap, or going for a light walk. Whatever form it takes, when you rest, you are dismantling that limiting belief that says, "My worth comes from what I do." Of course you're not going to fall into that trap right away. You've done a phenomenal job so far of internalizing who God says you are. But let me tell you how things will start to go left.

You're going to get so juiced on your talents that you might start taking all kinds of action. You know what you do well, and you're not afraid to use your genius. So you will. And it will feel awesome as grace goes before you. But the high you'll get from making an impact can become addictive, leading you back to the hamster wheel of industriousness. You'll like how it feels to get results. So you'll work a little harder. And when you do, you'll get even more positive feedback. So you'll work a little more. And then a little more. And the cycle will continue. Affirmation and impact start feeding your ego, until soon you've overused your talents and worked yourself to the point of burnout.

Chill. You are worth more than what you can produce. Rest, on purpose, to remind yourself of what it feels like to be valuable while doing nothing. This is a powerful and subversive act. Rest is resistance, as the Nap Ministry often says. You are declaring to the world, and to that little voice inside, that your value is not tied to your performance.

Make a plan to rest now. I like to tell my clients to frontload their schedule with PEP—physical, emotional, and psychological activities that lead to restoration. Go for a bike ride, listen to some music, or read the newspaper. Do whatever feels self-indulgent and helps you replenish as you lean into activities that do not leverage your talents.

Gratitude

The next posture, gratitude, is one of my favorites because it speaks to that anxiety that so easily slips into our hearts as we evolve. Gay Hendricks, the same guy who came up with the Zone of Genius concept, talks about the upper limit problem—or hitting the ULP.[3] It's that moment when we're about to do or become abundantly more than we've been, and we panic at the prospect of exceeding our old limitations. I find that just before hitting the ULP, my clients self-sabotage, fixating on all they lack and ignoring what they've already accomplished. Before long they sink under the despair of not yet being who they want to become.

Living out your purpose is a marathon, not a sprint. It takes time. Gratitude will help you celebrate along the way as it dismantles discouragement and worry. "Gratitude *is* optimism," *I Want to Thank You* author Gina Hamadey wrote. "It's choosing to see the contours of what's there instead of the shadows of what's missing."[4] Every time you say thank you, you celebrate the wins you've already achieved—and in so doing, remind yourself that you have what it takes to keep going. Gratitude gives you the confidence to break through the upper limit.

Ironically, gratitude also provides a critical skill you'll need for continued growth: humility. I don't know who needs to hear this, but you're not the master of the universe. The creation and maintenance of the world does not, in fact, rest on your shoulders. So with all the love in the world, I must tell you what my husband

and I say to each other when we notice the other person getting too bigheaded: "Don't go thinking you're so such-a-much." The world turns just fine on its axis without you.

Now, don't get me wrong; I want you to feel powerful and important. I want you to believe in yourself and take ownership over turning your dreams into reality. I mean, I'm the girl who has personally walked on fire with Tony Robbins while screaming, "If you can't, then you must!" So I'm here for it. Embrace your personal power. But it's important for your freedom that you stay humble. I don't want you trapped under the weight of trying to make everything happen for yourself. Keeping a posture of gratitude will remind you that much of life is something you receive, not just outcomes you create. And when you stop taking credit for everything you've attained in your life, you don't have to be so stressed about hustling to get what you don't have. You know the things you lack may not come from your effort. So you can exercise your agency and then let life play out as it will.

I encourage you to create some sort of daily gratitude posture. It can be anything from sending thank-you cards to acquaintances, writing a quick list of gratitude before bed, or calling up your parents to thank them for some lesson they've taught you. Lean into gratitude however it feels natural for you. The good life is a gift. Receive it and say thank you.

Generosity

The next posture of identity formation is generosity. It comes from a lesson my mother taught me when I was a little girl growing up in California. We didn't have a whole lot—we were your typical middle-class Black family living in apartments across the street from a wealthy gated community. But my mom always encouraged me to give what I had away to others. She would say, "Chanel, when you give something away, you create space for God to give you something new."

I don't know if she thought about it that deeply at the time, but my mom was teaching me a valuable lesson in detachment. She was training me to develop an abundance mindset before it was trendy. Because from my mom's perspective, there was always more to be had—more food, money, books, friends, etcetera. Even when we were out of money to pay rent, she expected God to provide. There would always be enough. And that expectation taught me that possessions are fluid, so we can hold them loosely.

I want you to grab that same message by choosing to live generously as you pursue your purpose. As you expand and acquire more, you'll be tempted to believe you are the summation of your possessions. And that lie will cause you to hoard and hold on to what you have, terrified you'll lose the ground you've gained. It's a form of bondage. I don't want you to belong to your belongings.

A posture of generosity reminds you how things move in and through your life like sand through a sieve. As you pass along what you've been given, you create space for more growth and blessing in your own life. So pour yourself out—continually give through random acts of kindness, financial resources, or a loving word someone needs to hear. Each act of generosity you commit will free you from being owned by the things you own.

Play

Lastly, we have reached the posture of play. And though it seems frivolous, an afterthought tacked on at the end, play may be the most important posture to lean into for purpose-driven women. Play reminds us not to take ourselves too seriously.

There is a certain level of gravitas to this business of calling. A lot is on the line as we talk about finding meaning in all five of those life buckets. You're eager to know why you exist so you can have more personal fulfillment. But you also want deeper intimacy in your relationships, you want a stellar career, you want to touch the fingertips of God through spiritual practices, and you want to change the world around you. Living a life of consequence matters.

And so, as you step out, implementing all you've learned in order to live with greater purpose, you might start to approach life with such sobriety that you forget you're meant to have fun. In Psalm 16:11, David said, "You make known to me the path of life; you will fill me with joy in your presence, with eternal pleasures at your right hand." I love the little reminder that the path of life leads to joy as we dance and play alongside God, stewarding the purpose we've been given.

Our last posture is to approach life with curiosity and wonder through play. It's not just about having a positive mindset. There are practical results we get from recreation too. Did you know that integrating more play into your life actually releases creativity? When we're having fun, we become more solutions-focused and open to possibilities. I used to work for a woman named Julie Morgenstern, who is a *New York Times* bestselling author and organizing expert. When I worked for her, Julie's business was booming and expanding—from her work as an author to designing organization products with FranklinCovey, to speaking all over the world, to serving as a consultant to major Fortune 500 companies.

It was during this time of growth, which included some stress as she ventured into new territories, that Julie started taking gymnastics classes in New York City to shake up her creativity. Flipping in the air and playing helped her find new solutions in her business, think of herself differently, and become more nimble to manage the obstacles that came her way. From watching her firsthand in the office, I can say for sure her ingenuity as a female business owner most often came from the time she spent playing. She thought outside the box, was willing to take risks, and was quick to assess if her professional pursuits were rooted in her internal passion or external pressure. Her brilliance in a strategy meeting was bolstered, not inhibited, by her commitment to have fun. Play expanded her horizons, and it can do the same for you.

LIFE STARTS NOW

Well, there you have it, friend. I'm tempted to keep writing because I don't want to end our time together. But I am confident you are set up for success, to discover the purposeful life God has for you to live. Continue leaning into the postures of silence, rest, gratitude, generosity, and play as you find your footing in the new life you're constructing for yourself.

I feel a bit like a mama bird, nervous to see you take flight for the first time and launch into all God has for you. But trust that you've got this. You don't need to search for significance because you already have it. Lift your head out of the shallow water and stand courageously in the woman you were created to be.

She's enough.

You're enough.

I can't wait to see the kind of life you'll design, rooted in your purpose, that will use your talents, honor your heart, and leverage the influence you have to participate in renewing the world. The road ahead may not always be easy or perfectly paved in the direction you're meant to go. But if you'll allow me an Oprah moment, here's what I know for sure: The ordinary life you live according to your purpose will always be more fulfilling than the extraordinary life meant for someone else. Trust in the path before you.

I pray the Lord will bless you and keep you as he sends his grace ahead of your steps to provide more courage, direction, and meaning than you ever imagined. Choose today to be the woman you already are. And don't wait one second longer, because there is no time to waste. You are made for such a time as this—so go live out your one wild and wonderful purpose.

Life starts now.

Acknowledgments

You know that moment when a movie ends and the credits start to roll? If you're like me, you start groping around in the dark, hunting for your purse and trying to ignore that sticky substance on the bottom of your shoes. It's disgusting, weird, and you kind of have to pee. Maybe you feel that way right now. But cram another fistful of popcorn in your mouth because the credits matter. Power through. These are the people who have put in the work behind the scenes, and they deserve their flowers. So let's make the ending of this book more like Broadway, less like Regal Cinemas. Join me in a standing ovation for the people who are in the credits of my life.

First, I want to thank Jesus for his loving kindness to make a way where there is seemingly no way. The four-year-old girl inside of me who sat teaching herself to read over a copy of *Cinderella* never thought she'd one day become Cinderella. But won't he do it! To God be the glory for doing a new thing in my life. Look, Mom and Dad. I made it!

Next, I am eternally grateful to my husband, Dr. Lanre Dokun. Babe, you "got it when it was lukewarm." There is no one else I'd want to share my life with than you. Thanks for believing in me and always saying, "We've got to get this girl in front of a crowd." You're my best friend and partner. Plus, you always have the perfect metaphor for the moment. How lucky can one girl get?

To my son, Aridunu, Mommy is so proud of the man you are becoming. Just the other day you painted a series of rainbow-colored windows against a white background. And when I asked what the picture meant, you said, "These windows are my feelings." I sat and thought about it for about thirty minutes. Now when I'm upset, I often think, *what color window am I feeling right now?* I'm in awe of your emotional intelligence and hope you carry it with you for life. I cannot wait for the impression you leave on the world as you step into your life's calling.

I know a thing or two about family after years of unpacking family systems theory in my training. But one thing I couldn't fully have learned in school is how there is family you are born into and there is family that you choose. Luckily, I have been blessed to experience both in abundance. I am grateful for the Graham and Paige families that laid the foundation for the woman I am now. I love you, Cordell, even though you called me a little Mussolini when I was seven years old (accurate), and I love you, Donovan, even though you do the most. Siblings are friends God picks for you. Thank you for being mine. Thank you also to the Parmentier-Ruiz and Dokun families. You fulfill God's promise to me that what has been taken will be restored twofold. I am grateful for the way you model his heart to me each day.

I have to thank my forever "framily"—the Life Group. I will always remember our motto: Life Group is for life. Thank you for your steadiness and unfailing love. I'm especially grateful for Blair, Steph, Amanda, and Hatz, who stand at the ready to thumb a response to any text I send. Let's keep doing life together, eh? Also sorry for my insanely long Marco Polos.

A big thanks to my other girlfriends who are like sisters from other misters. I love you Roo, Tiffany, Charisma, Victoria, Juliette,

Meghan, and Mademoiselle Stephanie. Thank you for giving my life color and context. Special shout out to Megan Jacobs and Kball who read every word of my manuscript before I sent it off to print. Your cheers, challenges, and concerns in the margins made this a better book for every woman. Thank you also to Ashley Abercrombie who midwifed this book out of me and helped me believe my voice matters! There should be a Netflix show of you reacting to other people's writing. Because I seriously wanted to record your feedback as you responded to every line of my book proposal. I cherish you! I'm also grateful for Rasheeda Winfield. Girl, we owe Jon Tyson a cigar for introducing us. Thank you for your wise humor and for always bringing me back to God's promises as we wrestle through life together. I don't know what I'd do without you as my #1 collaborator.

Speaking of JT, thank you, Jon, for being the kind of pastor who prays before you preach. My faith has been refined in the furnace of your biblical and cultural exposition. I have nothing but honor and gratitude for you. I also want to thank our old Trinity Grace Church community and the fam at Epiphany Church Brooklyn for running this race with me. A special thanks to Josh Staton, who first invested in me as a Life Planner and showed me what brotherly love looked like. Ninjas like you move in silence, but I see you, friend. Hug that beautiful wife of yours for me.

Hey, wouldn't it be cool if there was a community of people embodying the things I've talked about in this book and actively seeking to do good in the world? Oh snap, there is... big hugs to Jeff Shinabarger and the Plywood community for letting me sit on the board to help catalyze a community of startups. Together we can do better faster, and that is my jam! Alongside Plywood,

I'm grateful for the Renegade Global community. It's been a joy to partner with you in positive disruption, leading the way in human innovation work. Ajo, you always multiply my thinking tenfold, and I'm grateful for your leadership.

To be honest, there are a lot of meaningful people in my life, and I'm sure I'm forgetting someone important. Like duh—my publishing team! To be honest, this book would just be a really interesting Google doc or self-indulgent set of journal entries without a few key people. Thank you to my agent, Chris Park, whose sensitivity, vision, and camaraderie have changed my life. You are the real MVP. Thank you for teaching me to say less, expect more, and trust I am enough. Also thank you to my Nelson Books family. Thank you, Jessica Wong Rogers, for originally acquiring this book before you moved onto your next adventure. Thank you, Brigitta Nortker, for shepherding my manuscript through the process. In our first meeting I saw in your eyes that you fully got me. It's a privilege to have an editor who enhances not inhibits. Thank you for sprinkling your fairy dust of genius across every page.

Lastly, I want to thank all my past and present clients. The hard-won truths you've fought to discover and the insights you've come upon in your work are littered throughout these pages. Thank you for being women of consequence and fiercely living out your life purpose. Okay, let's get out of here and go live these incredible lives we've got waiting. I am with you and for you.

Notes

Chapter 2: The Problem with Chasing Significance

1. Will Storr, *Selfie: How We Became So Self-Obsessed and What It's Doing to Us* (London: Picador, 2018), 17.
2. Parker J. Palmer, *Let Your Life Speak: Listening for the Voice of Vocation* (San Francisco: Wiley, 2000), 10.
3. Derek Thompson, "Workism Is Making Americans Miserable," *Atlantic*, February 24, 2019, https://www.theatlantic.com/ideas/archive/2019/02/religion-workism-making-americans-miserable/583441/.
4. Gen. 2:18.
5. Gregg Easterbrook, *The Progress Paradox: How Life Gets Better While People Feel Worse* (New York: Random House, 2003), 171.
6. BLS Reports, "Consumer Expenditures in 2018," *US Bureau of Labor Statistics*, May 2020, https://www.bls.gov/opub/reports/consumer-expenditures/2018/home.htm.

Chapter 3: The Power of Your Daily Liturgies

1. Jefferson Bethke, *To Hell with the Hustle: Reclaiming Your Life in an Overworked, Overspent, and Overconnected World* (Nashville: Nelson Books, 2019), 7.
2. Jessica Stillman, "This Is How Reading Rewires Your Brain, According to Neuroscience," *INC.com*, February 22, 2021, https://www.inc.com/jessica-stillman/reading-books-brain-chemistry.html.
3. James K. A. Smith, *Desiring the Kingdom: Worship, Worldview, and Cultural Formation* (Grand Rapids: Baker Academic, 2009), 54.
4. Ron Marshall, "How Many Ads Do You See in One Day?," Red

Crow Marketing Inc., September 10, 2015, https://www
.redcrowmarketing.com/2015/09/10/many-ads-see-one-day/.

5. Mary Oliver, *Upstream: Selected Essays* (New York: Penguin, 2016), 8.

6. Gary Henderson, "How Much Time Does the Average Person Spend On Social Media?" *Digital Marketing Blog*, August 24, 2020, https://www.digitalmarketing.org/blog/how-much-time -does-the-average-person-spend-on-social-media.

Chapter 4: The Courage to Be Nobody

1. Dale Vernor, "PTSD Is More Likely in Women Than Men," National Alliance on Mental Illness, October 8, 2019, https://www .nami.org/Blogs/NAMI-Blog/October-2019/PTSD-is-More-Likely -in-Women-Than-Men.

2. Bessel A. van der Kolk, *The Body Keeps the Score: Brain, Mind, and Body in the Healing of Trauma* (New York: Penguin, 2014), 73.

3. Matt. 7:13.

4. J. D. Salinger, *Franny and Zooey* (New York: Little, Brown, 1961), 30.

5. Matt. 10:39.

Chapter 5: How to Reclaim the Morning

1. John Mark Comer, *The Ruthless Elimination of Hurry* (Colorado Springs: WaterBrook, 2019), 47.

2. Parker J. Palmer, *Let Your Life Speak: Listening for the Voice of Vocation* (San Francisco: Wiley, 2000), 4–5.

3. Allison Fallon, *The Power of Writing It Down: A Simple Habit to Unlock Your Brain and Reimagine Your Life* (Grand Rapids: Zondervan Thrive, 2021), 10.

4. Thomas Merton, *New Seeds of Contemplation* (New York: New Directions, 2007), 6.

Chapter 6: Redefining Your Purpose

1. Paul David Tripp, *New Morning Mercies* (Wheaton, IL: Crossway Books, 2014), 17.

2. *The Good Place*, season 3, episode 6, "A Fractured Inheritance," directed by Beth McCarthy-Miller, aired November 1, 2018, on NBC.
3. Jer. 29:7.
4. Dolly Parton (@DollyParton), "Find out who you are and do it on purpose. #Dollyism," Twitter, April 8, 2015, 2:40 p.m., https://twitter.com/dollyparton/status/585890099583397888.

Chapter 7: The Importance of Knowing Your Talents

1. Gay Hendricks, *The Big Leap: Conquer Your Hidden Fear and Take Life to the Next Level* (New York: HarperOne, 2009), 34.
2. Hendricks, *Big Leap*.
3. Shonda Rhimes, *Year of Yes* (New York: Simon & Schuster, 2015), xviii.
4. Andy Crouch, *Culture Making: Recovering Our Creative Calling* (Downers Grove, IL: InterVarsity Press, 2008), 257.
5. Crouch, *Culture Making*, 256.
6. Marianne Williamson, *A Return to Love* (New York: HarperOne, 1992), 190–91.
7. Carl Cederström and André Spicer, *Desperately Seeking Self-Improvement: A Year Inside the Optimization Movement* (New York: OR Books, 2018), chap. 12, Kindle.
8. Acts 16:13–15.
9. Est. 4:14.
10. C. S. Lewis, *The Weight of Glory: And Other Addresses* (New York: HarperOne, 2009), 26.
11. Est. 4:14.

Chapter 8: How to Find Your Flickers of Genius

1. *Office Space*, directed by Mike Judge (1999; 20th Century Fox).

Chapter 9: The Redemption of Your Life Story

1. Frederick Buechner, *Wishful Thinking: A Seeker's ABC* (New York: HarperOne, 1993), 119.

2. Christina Norman, "Maya Angelou Public Radio Special: Award-Winning Poet on Why Black History Month Still Matters," *HuffPost*, February 14, 2012, https://www.huffpost.com/entry/maya-angelou-radio-special-_n_1276463.

3. Stephen Madigan, *Narrative Therapy* (Washington, DC: American Psychological Association, 2011), 33.

4. Andy Crouch, *Culture Making: Recovering Our Creative Calling* (Downers Grove, IL: InterVarsity Press, 2008), 262.

Chapter 10: How to Activate Your Heart

1. Heb. 12:1.

2. Brené Brown, *Dare to Lead* (New York: Random House, 2018), 185.

Chapter 11: The Shift from Fear to Excitement

1. David Goldstein, "Walter Cannon: Homeostasis, the Fight-or-Flight Response, the Sympathoadrenal System, and the Wisdom of the Body," *Brain Immune*, May 16, 2009, http://www.brainimmune.com/walter-cannon-homeostasis-the-fight-or-flight-response-the-sympathoadrenal-system-and-the-wisdom-of-the-body/.

2. Regan Walsh, *Heart Boss: Trust Your Gut, Shed Your Shoulds, and Create a Life You Love* (Austin, TX: Houndstooth: 2021), 165.

3. Lam. 3:22–23.

Chapter 12: How to Steward Your Influence

1. *Merriam-Webster*, s.v. "stewardship," accessed June 1, 2021, https://www.merriam-webster.com/dictionary/stewardship.

2. Terence Lester (@imTerenceLester), "A huge part of growth is connected to humility. You have to humble yourself where you currently are in order to become the next best version of yourself. In other words, you have to give up something to grow." Twitter, May 5, 2021, 6:44 a.m., https://twitter.com/imTerenceLester/status/1389908764954873857.

3. *Arrested Development*, season 1, episode 2, "Top Banana," directed by Anthony Russo, aired November 9, 2003, on Fox.

4. Kate Harris, *Wonder Women: Navigating the Challenges of Motherhood, Career, and Identity* (Grand Rapids: Zondervan, 2013), 51.

5. Harris, *Wonder Women*, 52.

6. Oprah Winfrey, "What Oprah Knows for Sure About Making the Most of Every Minute," Oprah.com, accessed June 28, 2021, https://www.oprah.com/inspiration/what-oprah-knows-for-sure-about-making-the-most-of-every-minute_1.

7. Reid Wilson, *Stopping the Noise in Your Head: The New Way to Overcome Anxiety and Worry* (Deerfield Beach, FL: Health Communications, 2016), 137.

Conclusion: Swimming Lessons

1. John Mark Comer, *The Ruthless Elimination of Hurry* (Colorado Springs: WaterBrook, 2019), 125.

2. Comer, *Elimination of Hurry*, 126.

3. Gay Hendricks, *The Big Leap: Conquer Your Hidden Fear and Take Live to the Next Level* (New York: HarperOne, 2009), 15–16.

4. Gina Hamadey, *I Want to Thank You* (New York: TarcherPerigee, 2021), 189.

About the Author

CHANEL DOKUN is a certified Life Planner and Relationship Expert trained in Marriage and Family Therapy. She specializes in helping women step into their life's true calling through her Women of Consequence life-planning organization. Prior to running her own business and cofounding a seven-figure therapy practice, Healthy Minds NYC, she worked in publishing at Hearst Magazines. She now splits her time between New York City and Atlanta with her psychiatrist husband and son. Chanel's writing and contributions have appeared publications such as the *New York Times*, *Real Simple*, *Woman's Day*, *Essence*, Moneyish, *Christianity Today*, and *Relevant Magazine*.